South Pacific at Seventeen

USS Cofer (APD-62)
World War II

James Richard Snellen

Order this book online at www.trafford.com
or email orders@trafford.com

Most Trafford titles are also available at major online book retailers.

Print information available on the last page.

ISBN: 978-1-4251-3763-2 (sc)
ISBN: 978-1-4251-6871-1 (hc)

Edited by Danielle Amundson

Trafford rev. 08/25/2023

www.trafford.com

North America & international
toll-free: 844-688-6899 (USA & Canada)
fax: 812 355 4082

Dedication

My sincere thanks goes out to many, starting with my wife of 58 years, Dorothy L. (Stocker) Snellen. We were married February 12, 1949 on her 20th birthday.

I am also indebted to my parents, Herbert Snellen, Sr. and Sophia L. Whitesides Snellen. It is unfortunate that I did not put this in writing while they were alive so they could have known how much I loved and appreciated them both. Their direction, support and love will never be forgotten.

In addition, I would like to mention my sixth, seventh, and eighth grade three-room schoolhouse teacher, J. C. Brashear from Bullitt County, Kentucky who did so much to earn my deep respect. It is funny because while in school, I thought he was too demanding. He taught three grade levels in his one room— that's how things were done back then. I wrote him in the sixties letting him know how much I appreciated his strong way of teaching and guiding us in the right direction. I later learned that he really appreciated my letter.

My deep appreciation goes to several of my USS Cofer (APD-62) shipmates who I so appreciated both during my months aboard our ship and after. The one person who convinced me years ago to write a book was Captain Alvin P. Chester. He was in charge when I boarded the Cofer and was responsible for me receiving my first bronze star. He knows "I shall never forget."

There were sixteen men in our boat division and we all became close friends after the war. Edwin J. McClendon was the boat officer of our boat division. The Coxswain of our LCVP boat #2 was Walter J. Whitaker, who also became a close friend until his death. In addition, someone very special who was an expert in his position was L.J. Turley, First Class Signalman. He, like me, was from Kentucky and was already a seasoned veteran when I boarded the Cofer in New York. I was only seventeen years old at that time and, no doubt, he felt sorry for such a young, inexperienced fellow Kentuckian.

Last but not least, I would like to express my gratitude to Harvey "Scotty" Parrish, the Cofer's Gunnery Officer. When the war ended, there was no longer any need for our LCVP's boat division (Landing Craft Vehicle Personnel that put the infantry ashore). I was then transferred to Scotty's ordinance division and, thanks to this former Annapolis graduate, I left the ship as a Gunner's Mate, 3rd Class. He was very strict, but was one of the nicest officers anyone could have served under. Because of his time at Annapolis, I think he understood enlisted men. He, too, is a person I strongly consider a friend. I feel so honored that even years later, several former officers are kind to me. Remember, I was just a Gunner's Mate, 3rd Class enlisted man.

When I started this book years ago, many family members and friends never gave up pushing me to completion. Now, I certainly do thank all of them for believing that it could be done. My sincere appreciation goes to our daughter, Vicki Myatt and our grandson and granddaughter, Nick and Jill (Babski) Myatt who really got involved in helping. Our granddaughter, Danielle (Myatt) Amundson from Minnesota, who took my long scribbled manuscript and put it into type, is the one who deserves so much credit because she spent hours and hours editing and putting this together. No words can express my deep appreciation to Danielle.

Thanks to everyone for making this book a reality for me.

Author's Note

All dates, places, and events that I have included in this book are written to the best of my 80 year-old memory. Please remember that these events occurred more than 60 years ago. As I have written this book, I have continuously consulted the USS Cofer (APD-62) ship's log to ensure that I have the most accurate account as possible.

1

At 80 years of age, I am one of the youngest of all World War II veterans still alive. As the USS Cofer's historian and coordinator of our association, my role is to keep in contact with all of the shipmates whom we have been able to locate. I am writing this book to tell of my experiences aboard our ship, the USS Cofer (APD-62), in the South Pacific during World War II in honor of my fellow-comrades lost at sea, my shipmates who still attend yearly reunions, and my friends and family. In no way did I consider myself a hero—nor do I now. Even though I was awarded two bronze stars, the things that I did were the same things being done by countless others.

Never having attempted to undertake such a task as this, my writing will no doubt be less than professional. It is not intended to be an autobiography, but in order to tell what life was like before and during World War II, I found myself including many fond memories of my childhood growing up in Kentucky.

* * * * *

On September 27, 1926 I was born at home on Weaver's Run Creek in Bullitt County, Kentucky. I was named James Richard Snellen after both of my grandfathers—James, after my dad's father and Richard after my mother's father who passed away when my mother was only eleven years-old. Most people called me "Jimmy," but when my dad would get really mad, he would call me "Dick" for my middle name. I never really knew why. I was the second oldest of five boys and one daughter. Needless to say, (to no fault of hers), my sister was spoiled; or so we boys thought.

My grandfather, James "Jim" Franklin Snellen, had always been a farmer and owned the farm where I lived during most of my childhood. He always tried to encourage me to do what was right (possibly because I was named after him). My grandfather was special in every way—I looked up to him and loved him.

My grandmother, too, was special. She would take us swimming in Pond Creek, which was located at the back of our farm. I always remember the really big biscuits and special cakes she would bake for us. It's fun to see how certain items stand out in my memory, even years and years later.

I could tell so many, many stories about growing up on my grandparents' farm. We worked hard, yet we did not call it "work" because all children living around us worked the same way. Nobody complained; it was life. Even at a very young age, we had to get up early to milk six to ten cows by hand, feed the horses, the mules and the hogs—all before going to school. After school, we would use a crosscut saw to cut enough firewood to last us through the night. Then, we would do the feeding and milking again before supper.

My family lived in my grandparents' old log farmhouse (shown on the right) that had been built before the Civil War. We had no electricity or running water. Our water came from a deep-well pump, which meant that we always had very cold water. Washing the clothes was usually an all-day chore for my mother and grandmother. Once a week we would carry the wash water from the creek probably about one-eighth of a mile uphill to the house. After heating the water outside in a large iron kettle, the washing was done on a scrub board by hand. Then they ironed the clothes with metal irons that had been heated on the wood-burning cook stove.

Farmers in the area would often call on my brother and me to do many things from hoeing corn to picking green beans and peas—all major produce items in our area. Many times I hoed corn for fifty cents a day. But in the long summer days, I would hoe corn for twelve-hour days for the same fifty cents. Picking beans and peas was much better because they paid twenty-five cents a bushel to pick. However, this *was* considered work, and it was back-breaking.

Our major farm product was corn. Our farm produced some of the longest ears of corn of all of the farms in that area. Usually early in the year, backwater from early rains caused flooding in our corn fields, leaving rich top soil (and weeds) like you would not believe. We had to continuously hoe and hoe to keep the weeds out of the cornfields. During harvest time, two of us would gather corn by hand using a team of horses and a wagon that straddled one row of corn. We would each pick two rows from the wagon along with the row the wagons knocked down, usually gathering five rows at a time. We would then put the corn in the barn's corncrib, which was an old log building similar to our house.

I remember my grandfather would kill a number of hogs each year after fattening them on corn. To assist in the feeding, every so often a large tank truck would bring by-product from the Kentucky distilleries to sell to us to feed the hogs. This "mash" was a big thing back then to keep the hogs growing.

My grandfather also had one of the largest orchards in our county. He had 38 apple trees plus pear, peach, and cherry trees, which we had to keep picked and

This is a photo taken of my grandparents' log house around 1895 that I grew up in. (Left to right) On the mule is my Great Uncle James Washington McNutt, my Great Grandfather Jimmy McNutt, and my Great Grandmother Lucy Stibbins McNutt. Standing behind those two are my Great Aunt and Uncle, Lillian and Tommy William McNutt. The lady standing alone is my Great Aunt Susan McNutt and my Grandmother Martha McNutt Snellen. On her right is my Grandfather James Franklin Snellen holding my uncle Archie Snellen. The man standing on right is my Great Uncle Hampton McNutt.

7

shipped. Apples would bring fifty to seventy cents a bushel. We would always put a number of bushels in cold storage until Christmas time. Because we had no refrigerator, we would dig large holes in the garden and line the bottom with straw. Then we put potatoes, apples, and turnips in the holes, covered these items with straw, and spread dirt on top of the straw to preserve the fruits and vegetables during the winter months.

Aside from all this work, our mother would often make us go to church on Sundays. For fun, we would ride the horses and the mules, but only on Sundays. We never used saddles, it was "bare back" to us and we were taught to break horses—we were just tough. The mules, however, had razor backbones, which were tough on your bottom to ride. My brothers and I would race friends on our mules and horses, but again, only on Sunday afternoons because otherwise we were at school or working at home.

Speaking of riding, I remember the time my grandfather bought two Holstein bulls, which he "marked"—making them steers. To make a steer, you had to castrate the bull. My grandfather then decided to make oxen out of them for us. He made a yoke for the oxen to pull the firewood to the woodpile area. My brothers and I decided it would be good to break these oxen to ride. The one with the most white on him was a pushover to ride, but the other one was something else! He would throw us off as quickly as our bottoms would hit his back. So, we decided to put a rope around him next to his back legs and get on backwards. If he bucked, we could hold the rope; making it more difficult for him to throw us. With this approach, we finally broke him to ride.

One day that I remember well was when my cousin, Paul Snellen, and I (we were both very small for our age) each grabbed a cow's tail and hung on with our toes up off the ground. Both cows ran. (Earlier, the cows had gotten into the alfalfa patch—I should mention that eating all that green hay gave them the runs.) As it ran, the cow that Paul was hanging onto suddenly "let go." It was like a huge gush of water...but it wasn't water. It sprayed all over his face and head. He was crying as hard as he could cry, so I led him to the pond and dunked him several times to wash off his face and head.

Another time, we decided to overturn an old Model-T Ford that we knew had a bee's nest inside. We wanted to see what the cows would do with the bees nearby. As you can imagine, it turned out badly. The bees stung the cows and the cows headed for the watermelon patch, which was all grown up with weeds. The cows went straight through the fence to get to the tall weeds—no doubt to help against the stings. That herd of cattle destroyed our watermelon patch and messed up the fence, but in the meantime, my cousin also got stung badly. When our grandfather learned what we had done, he really blistered us—and rightly so!

As I look back on my childhood, my most bothersome memories are surrounded by the way that people were perceived according to their class status. I can think of a number of families (sad to say) who were considered "lower class," and not just because of the family they came from. These "low class" families were just as hard working and as nice as the rest of us in the area. This, thank heavens, does not exist today as it did in the 1920's and '30s.

We lived next to a wonderful African American couple (back then we called them "colored") who we called Aunt Cecilia and Uncle Ed. We dearly loved those two people. I honestly thought they were actually my Aunt and Uncle until the day my mother got a letter from my second grade teacher. She was concerned that I was telling everyone that I had a colored Aunt and Uncle. My mother tried to explain, but it made no difference—they were my Aunt Cecilia and Uncle Ed Shacklette. They were special; we loved them.

Amazingly, I never knew of any people in the farming area where we lived who ever got into any kind of trouble—not one person. The worst thing I can remember was when someone jumped out of a car in front of our farm, grabbed a live goose, jumped back in the car and took off. It was thought to be someone who we knew who didn't live in our community.

I could go on and on about my early years growing up on the farm, but I will change with this last comment...we worked hard. I have always considered this as a plus, not a negative.

I later started Nichol's School in Bullitt County, Kentucky. As mentioned earlier in my dedication, my teacher was the greatest. Mr. J. C. Brashear was tough. When I was in the seventh grade, I guess I thought I was cute—a real smart aleck. But I was never mean. I remember one cute girl whose first name was Linda. She would catch me at recess and kiss me; and I kissed back. My friends and I were not mean, just mischievous. Mr. Brashear paddled me four times and made me write 4,400 sentences in my seventh grade year. It was then that I realized how special he was and that I deserved everything I got.

After starting high school, I learned about the outside world. I was fifteen years old when the Japanese attacked Pearl Harbor on December 7, 1941. After that day, I was desperate to fight what we then called the "Japs"—now a derogatory name to use. We would go to the movies and all we would see and hear about the Pacific War was that the Japanese were inferior to our fighting men, had inferior equipment, and even had poor eye sight...what propaganda! The news media today would never expose such false stories.

For my sixteenth birthday, I took the necessary steps to join the Army Air Corps and was accepted. But they would not take me until I turned eighteen. I hated to wait until my eighteenth birthday, yet my parents would not sign the papers for me to enter the services. I was so mad at my mother and farther because I wanted to get in on the action before it was over.

During my third year of high school, I was passing every subject. But I could have done even better if my interests had been on my schoolwork. At the time, my interests lay more in getting into the service and girls; even though my older brother, Herb Jr., who was in the Air Force, kept pleading with me to stay home and remain in school.

While away, my brother left a beautiful 1937 Ford Sedan for me to use. As I remember, there was only one other boy in our high school who had a car. So needless to say, because of the car, I was very popular with the girls. To top off having a car, I also had gasoline. (My best friend's mother and stepfather lived on a small farm and had a tractor, which entitled them to much more gasoline. Gas rationing was being enforced at that time. If I remember correctly, my family was only entitled to three gallons of gas a week for pleasure driving and we couldn't buy tires, while a tractor received "R" stamps to purchase gasoline while "A" stamps were for non-essential use.) Anyway, due to the gasoline available from my friend, he and I always had dates with high school girls. Again, it was because of the car and not Jim Snellen. But I honestly do not believe I was ever refused a date while in high school!

One Sunday night, my best friend Charlie "Bill" Harris, two girls, and I decided to drive south from Louisville, Kentucky towards Fort Knox. Why we went to Fort Knox, I do not remember. When we reached West Point, Kentucky, which is about eight miles from Fort Knox, we decided we should turn back toward Louisville because it was getting late. At the time, I did not know that this decision would change both my life and the life of my friend Bill Harris.

The girls, whom we had dated before, were good friends and nice. They both lived on the same street, just a few blocks apart. My date's last name was Thompson and Bill's date's last name was Blair. Bill had gone out with his date many times. I won't mention their first names.

We turned off Dixie Highway 31-W to a side street in West Point. Unbeknownst to us, the town had run a water or gas line ditch across the street with no lights or barricades to mark the obstruction. Our car ran into the ditch in the middle of the street around midnight. The house lights in the surrounding area were out, so we could do nothing but sit there until daylight.

None of us phoned home. Why? To this day, I don't know. I would like to note, however, that nothing improper happened between the girls and us.

We sat in that car all night long and the next morning. After being pulled out of the ditch, both girls decided we should drop them in front of each of their homes and take off. They, no doubt, felt that they could explain their overnight absence to their parents best without us.

After dropping off the girls, I left Bill Harris at his home, finally arriving at my parent's house about 10:00 a.m. My mother and dad were relieved to see me, yet extremely mad. Dad had not gone to work that morning because one of his sons had been missing without any word and they were both worried to death. (As mentioned earlier, when Dad would get mad at me he called me "Dick.") I was a smart aleck because I wanted to get into the service and they would not sign my papers. So, when I stepped in the door, my Dad said, and I remember to this day with chills down my spine, "Dick, where in the hell have you been?"

I replied, "If you don't like it, why don't you sign my papers to join the Navy?'

He said, "Son, go get your papers!!"

At 1:30 that same afternoon, even though I was not yet 18 years old, I was sworn into the Navy. After my dad's response, I quickly phoned my friend, Bill Harris, and he told his mother that my parents had given me permission to join the Navy. His mother also agreed to sign his papers. We enlisted together on April 26, 1944 and immediately boarded a train for the Great Lakes Naval Training Station in the town of Great Lakes, Illinois.

It was seven months past my seventeenth birthday when I finally became a sailor. I was so proud—I wanted to see some action. I did not know any better!

Seventeen years-old, I was accepted into the United States Navy in 1944.

11

My best friend from high school, Charles W. "Bill" Harris, and myself. His mother's 1929 Ford is in the background.

Bill Harris at home on our seven day leave after completing Boot Camp.

2

When my best friend, Bill, and I enlisted, the Navy was rushing their new recruits through boat training. We completed our boat training in four weeks.

Boot camp was really rough. I remember the man who shared a bunk above me. He was a 44 year-old married man who had been drafted and probably had children. I felt so sorry for him because he would often cry at night. And here I was, so anxious to see military action! This shows the difference between a 17 year-old who knew no better, and a 44 year-old man with a family and responsibilities.

Every morning we were up at 4:00 a.m. to do calisthenics and swimming exercises outside. It was cold; very cold! But mostly we marched and marched and marched. The swimming was the easy part for me, having grown up near water. But for my friend Bill Harris, it was a different story. Bill was not able to pass his swimming test and the Navy told him he would not be allowed to go home on leave with our group unless he passed his swimming test. We were worried, so we agreed that I would take his test for him.

On the day of the test, I went to the pool using the name Charles W. Harris. Luckily, they did not ask me for identification. I jumped in and an instructor followed me around the pool with a stick over my head for me to grab if I got tired. I passed for Bill with flying colors. How dumb this was—and thank heavens I did not get caught! This certainly did not help Bill, but he and I were so pleased because he had qualified and we would be going home together.

After graduation from boat training, we were at liberty to go home on leave for seven days before returning back for further assignment. While on leave, Bill Harris and I had a ball! We dated two girls whom we had dated a number of times before. My date's last name was Parks and his date was her cousin. We really thought we were something—sailors home on leave! Sailors in Louisville, Kentucky were much different than sailors in areas such as New York or Norfolk. Because there was a big Army base at Fort Knox and the Air Force's Bowman Field, Louisville was filled with Army men—but there were almost no Navy men! So again, we really thought we were hot stuff. I should add that while on leave, Bill and I did not try to see the two girls we were out with on the night before joining the Navy. We were afraid to go near their parents!

After our few days of leave, we returned to Great Lakes for our first assignments. Bill Harris and I were extremely disappointed to be shipped to different locations. Bill went to Little Creek, Virginia for LST amphibious training, and I was sent to Fort Pierce, Florida for amphibious training in LCVP small landing craft. The LST ships (abbreviation for "Landing Ship, Tank") hauled motorized vehicles and other materials. The LCVP landing craft (abbreviation for "Landing Craft, Vehicle, Personnel" sometimes called "Higgins" boats) were small boats with two 30-caliber machine guns and four sailors: the coxswain, the engineer, one gunner, and one combined post—the signalman, ship-to-shore radioman and gunner. I wound up as the radioman, signalman and gunner.

Getting to Fort Pierce from Great Lakes took me three days by troop train. This was a long and tiresome trip. I traveled on a coal burning train that had straw seats and no air conditioning. When we stopped in Meridan, Mississippi, ladies were passing out cookies to the troops through the train windows. One pretty young lady stretched up to the window, kissed me, and gave me her name and address. We corresponded throughout my time in the South Pacific, but lost touch after I returned to the states. I often wonder about her now and unfortunately, I cannot remember her name. But she certainly made an impression on me.

Late that night, our troop train finally stopped in the town of Fort Pierce, Florida. We were welcomed in an unwelcoming way. I will never forget standing in line beside the train waiting for our bags and then being told to run in the sand with our sea bags, which were quite heavy. Actually, from the moment of arrival at Fort Pierce, we were treated like dirt.

The island off of Fort Pierce where we were to be living for several months was called "Causeway Island." Today this island is totally developed with hotels and motels. But back then—it was a jungle. It was a lousy place to spend any time. The rumor was that Eleanor Roosevelt had selected it for an amphibious training base. As I remember, everybody hated the place, but I suppose it was a good place for training for the South Pacific.

Now that I look back, I wish I had kept a diary for every day that I was in the Navy. The stories about our Fort Pierce amphibious naval training would have been something to put into writing! To me, that place was the closest to hell that I ever hope to experience. The mosquitoes were awful during the day. When you were outside the tent, you would continually be slapping your arms and face killing mosquitoes. At night, we used mosquito netting over our cots. The tents we lived in had wooden floors and walls made of three feet of wood siding ending with screen and tarpaulin covers. The tents were set up for two four-man LCVP boat crews. Each boat crew slept on separate sides of the tent.

On the morning of our arrival I was elected to sweep and mop the wooden floor of our tent, probably because I was the youngest and the shortest. Everybody picked up their shoes so I could mop under their cots except for one person who was on our side of the tent—one of our own boat crew. His name was William E. Flippo from Coffeeville, Mississippi, our boat crew gunner. He remained on the cot, half asleep. When I asked him to please pick up his shoes so I could mop under his cot, he said, "If you want them up, you pick them up yourself!"

I grabbed the sides of his cot and flipped him onto the floor. He in turn jumped up and started to swing a punch at me but then suddenly started to smile and reached over to shake my hand. Later we called him "Flip" for Flippo. Flip became my best friend from that day until we separated for discharge from the Navy.

While at Fort Pierce, our boat crew trained and trained on the procedure for landing troops on the beaches. An LCVP (Landing Craft, Vehicle, Personnel) boat was able to haul up to 35 men and one officer. The boat was all wooden frames, except for the steel ramp in the front of the boat, and was powered by a General Motors diesel engine. My position was at the rear of the boat on the right side where I handled the ship-to-shore radio, the gun and signals to the main ship and other boats.

When our LCVP boat would hit a beach, we would drop the ramp to permit the troops or vehicles to depart. Then the engineer and I would crank the steel ramp back up. It took several minutes to crank the ramp back to the upright position, and then we would rush forward and connect the catches to lock the ramp as we backed off the beach.

During training, our boat crew practiced firing at targets that were towed behind planes by using the 30-caliber machine guns mounted on our boats. We had to wear our Mae West life jackets—named so because they were big around your chest. You could not sink with one on unless it became water logged due to damage. During practices, when we reached the mile and a half location from the beach, our officers would yell for us to abandon ship. After hitting the water, we had to take off our big sand shoes, tie them around our necks, and start swimming toward the beach. If the tide was going out, it was not an easy task.

One of the worst experiences that I can recall about Fort Pierce was the tear gas drill. Everyone was given a gas mask and told not to put it on until told to by our instructor. They threw cans of gas into the group and we took much punishment before they gave the order to put on the masks. It was evil, but necessary before the training course was completed.

In the evenings during training, we would purchase beer we called "green beer." Apparently, it was a beer that had been quickly made and bottled, maybe just for servicemen. One night I must have had one or two too many, because the next morning I was so sick. At muster, or roll call, I dropped out requesting permission to go the sick bay. I went to the tent where the pharmacist was located. I told the pharmacist there that my upset stomach was probably caused from the green beer I drank. He put the bottle back and got one down that read "castor oil." I said, "No way will I take that!" I had had too much of that at home as a small child. After he threatened to report me, I drank it. But, to this day, I still remember how sick I was at both ends—my last time to ever take castor oil.

After a few weeks, a call suddenly came out that the Navy needed volunteers for submarine duty. They promised a few days of leave if you were willing to join. I would have done anything to get away from Fort Pierce, so I volunteered. But I was turned down because they said I was too close to completing my amphibious training to be accepted. In hindsight, this was probably a real blessing after I saw how small a submarine really was—and not to mention the low survival rate! I have always felt that I was so lucky not to have been put aboard a sub, even though it was disappointing at the time.

My position was behind the right gun at the back of a LCVP boat similar to this one.

On September 11, 1944, after five months, we finally completed our LCVP amphibious training and we received orders to proceed to New York City for assignment aboard the USS Cofer (APD-62).

The USS Cofer (APD-62) had originally been the DE-208. She was originally built to escort troop ships, merchant ships, and others across the Atlantic Ocean. Her role would normally be to zigzag in front, at the sides, and behind a convoy of ships to protect the slow-moving ships against the German U-boats while crossing the Atlantic. The commanding officer was Lieutenant Commander Alvin P. Chester, USNR, former Commanding Officer of the USS EC Daily (DE-17). At the time of our arrival, the Cofer was in the process of being converted to the APD-62 (Attack Personnel Destroyer) for amphibious duty against Japanese suicide planes and other threats in the South Pacific. She was 306 feet in length, able to hold 12 officers and 190 enlisted men in addition to our four LCVP boat crews. The Cofer had one 5-inch, 38-caliber gun, three 40-mm guns, three 20-mm guns, and depth charges.

(A complete record of the Cofer's history before our boat crew came aboard is included in the Appendix.)

This is a replica of an LCVP landing craft that is now in the National World War II Museum.

This photo of the USS Cofer (APD-62) was taken in Leyte, Philippines in 1944. Our LCVP boats can be seen midship stacked two on each other.

3

Upon leaving Fort Pierce, our boat crews received orders to report aboard the USS Cofer—newly named the APD-62. It is important that I list all 16 men in our boat crew because we were the ones who were new to the Cofer. We were to man the four LCVP (Landing Craft Vehicle Personnel) boats, which would put assault troops ashore on the enemy beaches in the South Pacific.

The officer for our four boat crews was Ensign Edwin J. McClendon, US Navy Reserve. The crew breakdown under our officer McClendon was as follows:

Crew #2301	Responsibility—Rating	Rating Stands For
Scaffide, Joe F.	Coxswain – SIC	Seaman, First Class
Ehling, John W.	Signalman – SIC	Seaman, First Class
Dehart, Royal A.	Gunner – SIC	Seaman, First Class
Santone, Mario	Engineer – MoMM3/C	Machinist, 3rd Class

Note: Santone was the only boat crewman rated as high as 3rd Class; all others were rated the same as when leaving boot camp.

Crew #2302	Responsibility—Rating	Rating Stands For
Whitaker, Walter	Coxswain – SIC	Seaman, First Class
Snellen, James R.	Signalman – SIC	Seaman, First Class
Flippo, William E.	Gunner – SIC	Seaman, First Class
Crippen, Gilbert D.	Engineer – FIC	Fireman, First Class

Crew #2303	Responsibility—Rating	Rating Stands For
Moore, Alford T.	Coxswain – SIC	Seaman, First Class
Wajerski, Joseph E.	Signalman – SIC	Seaman, First Class
Dehart, Vinson	Gunner – SIC	Seaman, First Class
Mead, Garold D.	Engineer – FIC	Fireman, First Class

Crew #2304	Responsibility~ Rating	Rating Stands For
Smith, Clarence M.	Coxswain – SIC	Seaman, First Class
Beasley, Albert	Signalman – SIC	Seaman, First Class
Teague, Charles L. Jr.	Gunner – SIC	Seaman, First Class
Kolthoff, Arlo R.	Engineer – FIC	Fireman, First Class

Each boat had one coxswain who drove the boat and a gunner who manned a 30-caliber machine gun directly behind the coxswain. There was also one signalman, radioman and gunner who manned the 30-machine gun in the boat on the starboard side of the boat. Last but not least was the engineer, responsible for keeping the boat in perfect operating condition. The main responsibility for the engineer was the diesel engine. (If I remember correctly, these engines were built by General Motors. While you were riding in the boat, the stink from this engine was overwhelming! To this day, I cannot stand the smell of diesel fuel.) Again, my assignment was the combined duty of the signalman, radioman, and gunner.

Once we were accepted aboard the Cofer, our boat crew was sent to apartments that the Navy had leased on Myrtle Avenue in Brooklyn, New York. We lived in these apartments for several weeks while our ship was being converted in the Todd Shipyard's dry dock. What I remember most was that the apartment was very close to the elevated trains on Myrtle Avenue and the girls on the trains would wave and scream at the sailors. Of course, we waved and screamed right back.

As mentioned earlier, my closest friend was William E. Flippo from Coffeyville, Mississippi. We were in the same boat crew and he was just a little older than I. My next best friend was Charles L. Teague, Jr. from Waco, Texas, who we called "Chuck." Another close friend was Joseph E. Wajerski from Chicago. The three of us, plus another person who often joined us by the name of Arlo R. Kolthoff, really made the rounds in New York City.

While we waited for our ship's conversion, our only requirement was to be present for muster at the assigned time in the morning and then we were free until the next morning. After being under the extreme restrictions of Navy training for five months, our close boat crew took advantage of our free time in the big city. We only had 16 days in New York before boarding our ship and sailing to the South Pacific, so day and night we would go out on the town, getting very little sleep. New York, at that time, was a wonderful liberty town. I cannot remember what we did for money, but for service men, fares were half price and someone was always buying us a drink or a meal. This was World War II and the people supported the troops 100%!

One memorable day was spent at Coney Island where we met girls and rode different rides for much of the day. I met a beautiful young Italian girl from Ozone Park. Afterwards, we really hit it off and were together as much as possible before our ship left. We wrote regularly while I was in the South Pacific.

Back then, the biggest danger to sailors was (as we called them back then) the "queers," now known as gay men. In the short time that we were in New York City, more than one of our shipmates were raped by, as I remember, a pair of gay men. I remember one night when a shipmate came back to the apartment all bruised up after having been kissed and kissed over and over. He looked horrible. A day or two later, along with a buddy, he returned and trashed the apartment where he had been held. A bulletin was published for all of us to see, warning us not to go out alone at night because gay persons were targeting sailors. This type of crime was shocking to me, coming from the country. Before New York, I had only known of one gay couple back home.

While awaiting our ship's conversion, I heard from my older brother who was in England in the 8th Air Force. He had previously been stationed at the Windsor Locks Air Base in Connecticut and suggested that I contact a girl who he had dated from Hartford. So, Flippo and I made several trips by train from Grand Central Station to Hartford. My brother's friend arranged a date for Flip and the four of us went out. We went out several times and had a ball—we would arrive in Hartford about 5:00 p.m., eat, usually go to a movie, and leave Hartford around midnight, arriving at our Naval temporary station in time for morning muster. We always made it.

I wish I could remember exactly how many trips Flippo and I took to Hartford, Connecticut, but I do still remember the young lady Flippo met and went out with each time we went there. She really fell for Flippo and was so different than him—he was a real country boy from the very, very small town of Coffeyville, Mississippi and she was the daughter of a big city attorney. Regardless, she really fell for him and in writing while in the South Pacific, she kept him informed of her deep feelings for him. How they finally broke it off, I don't remember. But after he was discharged, he returned to Mississippi and married a nice girl by the name of Martha.

I purposely did not mention the names of the girls whom I met while in the service because I wouldn't want it to somehow be embarrassing for them if my story ever were to be published. Yet, not one girl that I dated or mentioned was ever, in anyway, anything but 100% nice. Never did anything happen to me that I was ashamed of in any way with any of the girls listed in my book....this is a fact.

Being a country boy from Kentucky, exploring New York and having a chance to go up in the Empire State Building was really an experience for me. This was about the same time that the military plane flew into the Empire State Building. I cannot remember if it was just before or just after my visit, but I know it was about the same time that I was there. At this time it was the tallest building, by far, in the U.S., and a real tourist attraction. Also, my friends and I made several visits to Time Square. I remember a big Chesterfield cigarette advertisement in the "Y" section of Times Square, which was fascinating to me—it even blew smoke. I wish I would have kept a diary of my time in New York because I am now writing most of this from memory.

I was not the only one enjoying myself while in New York awaiting the Cofer's conversion. Before moving on, I must include a story written by my boat officer, Lieutenant McClendon entitled "The Facts about the Purloined Piano." This story was written a few years back about the several Cofer officers who decided that the ship needed a player piano on board before leaving for duty in the South Pacific. I have included it because it tells the true story of how our small APD came into possession of a piano...

> When the Cofer was on her second trip to North Africa, a small group of crewmen who had musical instruments onboard got a pretty good band going. They felt what they needed most was a piano. Our former engineering officer helped start a fund, collecting money, and getting interested band members to serve as a committee to find and buy a used piano when the ship got to New York (where we were going to be converted to an APD).

> In New York...the officers and crew were moved off the Cofer. During this period, the band committee soon found a piano and got the price reduced to the funds they had available. They told the dealer that they could not take possession and move the piano aboard ship until the APD conversion was complete. At first the dealer agreed, but as the time for paying and picking up the piano went on, he began to waffle on the price and finally said the price would have to be some figure like $350—money they just didn't have.

> There seems to be a great deal of misinformation getting into print about a "liberated" piano from an aircraft carrier. I think the carrier was the USS Bennington, but to keep known facts clear, it will just be called "the Carrier" in this statement. In a recent account attributed to Lewis M. Andrew, Jr., the fact is that the USS Cofer...was the ship, which received the "stray" piano...

> A former engineering officer of the Cofer was aboard the Carrier, as observer, studying the ship's procedures and problems with shakedown for the new ship. The understanding was that he was scheduled to be assigned to a new carrier that was then under construction. At our Captain's invitation, he came over for dinner the first night while the Carrier was in port. The Carrier was moored at the same pier

as the Cofer (opposite side and some 30-40 yards down). After dinner, many of the officers stayed around to chat with this old friend. One of the numerous questions he was asked was, "How are things going aboard the new Carrier?" His rather lengthy answer could be summed up as a terrible case of "she is not ready for sea yet, much less for combat!"

After we finished the discussion about the Carrier's problems, our former engineering officer (guest) asked whether we had acquired our piano yet. We had to tell him the sad story of why we still had no piano. "Maybe," he said, "you should 'get' the piano from the Carrier! You should know they have a real good one in the junior officer's mess—ever since I have been aboard, no one has played it. It is a player piano with many rolls of popular music, yet no one plays it." The whole group began laughing about what a great "coup" it would be to get the Carrier's piano. (Our Captain had heard a rumor about our plans—he dismissed it completely.)

The group involved asked for volunteers. The Cofer had a young and inexperienced assistant engineering officer who seemed to be doing a fine job in the engineering room; he also had a great sense of humor. He then stood up and said, "I volunteer." Almost everyone laughed and then the discussion ended as we all had work to get to and our guest thanked everyone and started his return to the Carrier. One Cofer officer contended that he (our visitor) said to our assistant engineer, "I'll see you tomorrow."

The Cofer's Senior Engineering Officer had not sat in on the after-dinner session, pleading much work to do. Recognizing that he hadn't known the former Engineering Officer since they had not been on the Cofer at the same time, no one thought much about his early departure. They might have had little to discuss.

The following day, however, the Senior Engineering Officer from the Cofer helped his young assistant get shipyard work order forms and fill them out, ordering the removal of the piano from the Carrier to be repaired and tuned in the yard instrument shop. The orders were done and the inevitable extra copies were made, complete with fake illegible signatures, of course. The Officer on Deck on the Carrier almost certainly received one of these.

The Assistant Engineer knew he was going to need help getting the piano off the Carrier so he took a work party of volunteer crewmembers with him. The Officer on Deck on the Carrier sent a messenger to show the work party where the piano could be found. He also offered to help in getting the piano down the gangway from the second deck. This help was needed and accepted. Several senior officers waited at the gangway for the piano to exit the Carrier. No one seemed moved to ask why they would need all the rolls to repair and tune the instrument.

It should be noted that the Senior Cofer Engineer must have known what was *going on and had joined in the joke. All the events involving getting the piano off the Carrier occurred between 1600 and 2000 hours. Certainty about these events and times when they happened is based on having been Officer on Deck on the Cofer at that time. The writer even noted in the ship's log the fact and the time when the work party left and retuned to Cofer.*

The young engineer of this game had planned well—he had waited until near dusk to take his work party to the Carrier and to return as quickly as feasible with the piano, a bench, and the player rolls; all to the Carrier. As soon as the work party cleared the Carrier, they moved the piano and other items to a spot just aft the Cofer's stern. The Cofer's Officer on Deck and his messenger cleared a spot on the dock to provide a safe place for leaving the object of our affection.

Later, I simply cannot remember when we raised the "box" out of the hold. It could have been at Panama, Galapagos, or Bora Bora. I do recall the piano being stored on the main deck on the port side in the most forward section of the troop compartment. It was in excellent condition when we raised it from the hold and it did not seriously need tuning. I also know the band played it, giving much enjoyment to the entire ship's company.

Sometime later when the Carrier arrived in Leyte Gulf, after the Cofer and her crew had been fighting the war in that area for some five to six months, a message came over from the Carrier implying that if we did not "surrender" the piano, we could be in danger of some kind of attack. We replied that we knew nothing of what they spoke about and thus could not make a reply. The piano stayed on the Cofer and lived happily thereafter. I think the piano may have been given to a non-commissioned officer's recreation center in Florida.

This little account is dedicated to the band members, the work party, and the now deceased assistant engineer of the Cofer.

This piano, in fact, was donated to a church or an NCO club in Green Cove Springs, Florida in 1946. This later made one fun Navy story—even years and years after the war.

Finally, our ship was ready and our boat crewmen and officers boarded the USS Cofer. The Cofer sailors and officers who had previously been the crew for the DE-208 resented what the Navy had done to their beautiful ship. It was first built as a Destroyer Escort (DE) to escort ships across the Atlantic. When converted to an APD (Attack Personnel Destroyer) she was now taking on 17 additional amphibious crewmembers—our four LCVP (Landing Crew, Vehicle, Personnel) boat crews. We quickly saw that we were not welcome. In fact, we were outcasts to the old crewmembers. However, after our LCVP crews made our first couple of invasions, the attitude suddenly shifted from bitterness to deep respect for the LCVP crews who hit and delivered troops to the enemy beaches. All together, we made 11 total invasions in the South Pacific; 8 in the Philippines and 3 in Borneo.

As I am writing this memoir of my time in the Navy, I am simultaneously consulting the ship's complete log. While on duty, the Officer on Deck would log all of the daily events during his duty in the ship's log. The Captain later signed off on each day's 24-hour period. I have taken the following passages and combined them with my personal memories to reconstruct my time in the South Pacific...

Wednesday—September 27, 1944

The Cofer had completed her conversion and we were finally able to get underway. I was now a sailor and I thought I was hot stuff. Today was my 18th birthday! I celebrated my birthday while the Cofer sailed between New York City and Norfolk, Virginia. I remember singing a few popular songs back then for my birthday like "Anchors Away," "Bell Bottom Trousers," and "Praise the Lord and Pass the Ammunition."

The Cofer entered the Chesapeake Bay, Virginia and a Navy tug assisted us in docking. While we tied up alongside the USS Newman (APD-59), several additional enlisted men reported aboard today.

Thursday—September 28, 1944

Even after being in New York for as long as we were, we received 168 bags of mail today!

I was given one night of liberty in Norfolk. It was exciting for me to see all of the ships and to be in another part of the country I had never seen before. My friends and I took some pictures together to send home while walking around town and I distinctly remember seeing several signs posted saying "No dogs or sailors allowed." Norfolk was an old Navy town. They, no doubt, had had their fill of unruly sailors.

Saturday—September 30, 1944

We got underway at 0615 hours in formation with our five sister ships, known as the Comtrans Division #103: the USS Newman (APD-59), USS Liddle (APD-60), USS Kephart (APD-61), and the USS Lloyd (APD-63). Other ships joined our division when leaving Norfolk. They were all APD ships, but not from our division.

Before leaving the Norfolk Channel, our captain, Lieutenant Commander Alvin P. Chester, USNR, wanted to make sure everything and everyone aboard the Cofer was ready. He ordered all guns, powder magazines, and you name it checked, tested, etc.

At 1815 hours, we encountered rough seas off Cape Hatteras, North Carolina. Cape Hatteras is known for its really rough seas in stormy weather and over the years, many ships have been lost off this cape. This was only my second day at sea aboard a ship—ever! At Fort Pierce during amphibious training, we would usually go out about one and a half miles in our small LCVP Landing Craft, but never before had we experienced such rough stormy weather as we hit on this day.

When we first hit this rough weather, the Cofer was going up and down and rolling from side to side. Many of the ship's crew were already seasick from the day before. If you were among the seasick bunch, you were called "Land Lovers," but if you were a seasoned sea veteran, you were called an "Old Salt." Foolishly, I considered myself an "Old Salt," but was in for a surprise. While on deck, all it took was for the strong winds to carry the stench of someone upwind throwing up and I lost it. I joined the seasick bunch and I was sick for two days.

After recovering from that first bout of seasickness, I once again felt that I was now a veteran to rough seas. Believe me, our ship, which had formerly been built as a Destroyer Escort, was really violent in rough seas. It was nothing for one-forth or one-third of the front of the ship to go under water and then pop up, shake, and go back down again. Our bunks were one piece of heavy canvas lashed to a tubular pipe with four bunks stacked on top of each other. Many times in rough seas, the only way you could stay in your bunk was to lie on your stomach, lock your toes around the pipe edge, and hold on with your hands. This made for rough sleeping.

Sunday—October 1, 1944
We were heading for the Panama Canal, traveling at 20 knots. Almost daily, we were continuously having all sorts of drills to be ready. We were even having boat drills to practice abandoning ship.

Wednesday—October 4, 1944
Finally at 1700 hours, we reached the Panama Canal Zone and a canal pilot came aboard to steer us through the canal. At 1921 hours we were inside the first lock named the Gatun Lock and by 2010 hours, we were underway toward the next Pedro Miguel Lock.

At 2320 hours we had passed through the second lock, heading toward a series of the two Mira Flores Locks.

Thursday—October 5, 1944

At 0045 hours, we arrived and tied up at Pier #1 in the Balboa Canal Zone, Panama. We had one night's liberty in Panama City. This was some liberty town then—and believe me, anything and everything was in order! In Panama, anything could be bought with the American dollar. What President Bill Clinton and Monica Lewinsky did undercover was promoted on every main street—and it was all offered in the open—even yelled out. It was something like I have never seen since.

James Richard Snellen

Walter Whitaker, the Coxswain of our LCVP boat #2—a very special friend to me.

Below: Coney Island, New York in September of 1944. (lefft to right) William E. "Flip" Flippo, Charles "Chuck" Teague, and me, Jim Snellen.

Above: Another Coney Island photo of Flippo, Teague, and myself.

Below: John Ehling, Signalman, 3rd Class on LCVP boat #1 with myself on the right.

My friend, Charles Teague, from our boat division's LCVP boat #4.

My second Gunnery Officer aboard the Cofer, Scotty Parrish.

4

Saturday—October 7, 1944
At 1022 hours, the Cofer was underway from Panama, heading towards Hollandia, New Guinea sailing with the 7th Fleet. Today we really expended our ammunition in test firing. Captain Chester wanted us to be ready!

Monday—October 9, 1944
We crossed the equator and commenced ceremonies in accordance with the Navy tradition of the "Ancient Order of the Deep" initiation for sailors, nicknamed "Polywogs," who had never crossed the equator. What you would think should be fun was anything but! One officer even got a broken arm from it—the seasoned sailors did almost everything you could think of to us. One incident most memorable to me was crawling through a canvas-made tunnel with the ship's fire hose spraying water in my face. Waiting at the end of the tunnel was our chief. (He was a Philippine native who later deserted our ship when we arrived in the Philippines). After fighting the water pressure to get to him through the tunnel, I was told to kiss the chief's navel—all greased up with black grease. I brought my closed lips very close to his navel when someone unexpectedly shocked me with a charged cattle prod. Needless to say, my mouth flew open and did I ever kiss his dark greasy navel! It was one long, long, rough day for those of us who had never crossed the equator before. Now we were true "Shellbacks."

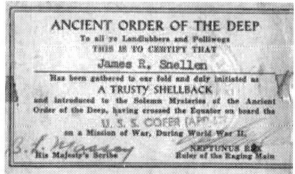

My Ancient Order of the Deep certification. I received this when I crossed the Equator in October of 1944 while en route to New Guinea.

Our next stop was the Galapagos Islands and this was a stay I will never forget. Captain Chester decided to put our four LCVP boats in the water as a drill. This was our first time ever to be lowered into the ocean from the Cofer. My boat was labeled number two out of the four LCVP landing craft aboard the Cofer. Our Coxswain, Walter Whitaker, was also the captain and in total charge of the boat. William E. Flippo was a gunner whose 30-caliber air-cooled machine gun mount was directly behind the steering wheel. As the Signalman, I manned the other machine gun, as well as handling the ship-to-shore radio and hand signals. Last aboard was the Engineer, Gilbert D. Crippen, otherwise known as our machinist's mate. It was his responsibility to keep our boat in perfect condition.

Because the water was so clear, we could easily see down deep. When our boat hit the water, we were in for a shock from the sharks swimming all around our boats. This turned out to be a worthwhile exercise, but the sharks were terrifying. I had never heard of the Galapagos Islands before landing there, but in later years I learned much about this special place. The tortoises are something there, plus the many types of rare birds. Our ship's log shows us stopping at the Seymour and Daphne Islands. Supposedly, pirates, convicts, scientists, etc. have all visited these islands. I have read many stories about Galapagos and I have always searched for comments about the sharks living there. But much to my surprise, I have never seen any mention of the sharks.

Friday—October 20, 1944
Our next stop was Fanui Bay, Bora Bora. We stopped there for refueling while en route to New Guinea. For me, Bora Bora was a dream island—the kind of island shown in the movies. To this day, I have never seen an island as beautiful as Bora Bora. Even now, after all the places I've been, I would give anything to revisit Bora Bora. The natives came out to greet our ship in their small boats. To us sailors, those dark-skinned girls were absolutely beautiful! I bought a grass skirt and sent it home to my cousin, Roma Hilbert, in Louisville, Kentucky. Roma and several of her high school friends took photos wearing the grass skirt and then mailed them to me. One of these girls, Rose Hepperle, later married my older brother, Herbert Snellen, Jr.

Saturday—October 21, 1944
After refueling, we left Bora Bora for Finschaven, New Guinea.

Sunday—October 22, 1944
While en route at 1130 hours, our ship stopped her engines and mustered all

aboard to observe a burial service aboard our sister ship, the USS Newman (APD-59). Four minutes later we resumed at 14 knots. This was the first time I had heard of anyone being buried at sea. Later, however, our ship experienced too many burials at sea. When buried at sea, the body was sewn into a sail cloth that had been weighted down. The Captain would say a few words about the deceased, as the body was slid overboard with the final words from the Captain, "I now commit this body to the deep." It was always a sad and touching experience.

Tuesday—October 31, 1944
Today an unidentified plane was picked up on radar. This was my first experience being called to General Quarters—showing us that we were now in the Pacific War Zone. When General Quarters were sounded, all hands went to man their battle stations. This happens within minutes—the men sleep in their clothes and everything except their shoes. The troops must be at their assigned battle stations within minutes or sooner, if possible.

Before sunrise and before sunset, we also manned our battle stations each and every day while in a war zone because the Navy believed most enemy attacks would come at sunrise and sunset. In addition to these times, we had battle station duty every four hours around the clock with eight hours off. This meant that one-third of the ship's crew were at their battle stations at all times. If you had the 2400 hour to 0400 hour watch, you were off only until one hour before sunrise when you had to be at General Quarter stations again. So, you often got only one or two hours of sleep before having to be back to your battle station for at least another hour. Needless to say, none of us ever got much sleep.

Wednesday—November 1, 1994
At 0620 hours we dropped anchor at Langenak, New Guinea and by 1030 hours we pulled anchor heading for Dreger Bay, New Guinea for refueling. We took fuel from a Danish ship, the SS Aase Marske. As always, when underway, we had daily drill exercises—our Captain Alvin P. Chester wanted to make sure we were ready when required.

Saturday—November 4, 1944
We dropped anchor in Humbolt Bay, New Guinea.

Monday—November 6, 1944
We transferred thirty Seamen, 2nd Class passengers that we had brought with us from the States.

Monday—November 13, 1944
In Hollandia, New Guinea, we did landing boat drills for the second time. We all knew that we would soon be involved in the "real thing." I never realized how unaware I was as to what was coming. I could not wait—I wanted to see action! This was what I had forced my parents to sign my papers to join the Navy for. How foolish I was!

Wednesday—November 14, 1944
Today we went through more landing boat drills. Our LCVP boat crews drilled and drilled for more than four hours before being hoisted back aboard the Cofer. We felt like we were ready for the real thing and we all knew it would come to us very soon.

Friday—November 17, 1944
Finally, we got underway from Hollandia, New Guinea en route to Leyte Island in the Philippines. Our convoy included a variety of LSM (Landing Ship Medium type amphibious assault ships), LST (Loading Ship, Tank), merchant ships, DE (Destroyer Escorts), PC (Patrol Craft otherwise known as submarine chasers), and other APD ships similar to the Cofer. Everybody was tense, but it seemed like we were all ready. Maybe I felt this way because I was so anxious to see some action.

While in route to Leyte, we drilled night and day, firing every weapon aboard the ship in an attempt to be ready. We were only traveling at 9 knots, because the LCMs and merchant ships in our convoy were very slow. The Cofer was able to move at 23 knots and the painfully slow speed of 9 knots left us vulnerable to Japanese submarines. As an APD (Attack Personnel Destroyer), the Cofer's role was to zigzag in a screening position for the entire convoy. Some zigzagging was also done by the other DE and APD ships in our convoy.

Our first night en route to Leyte was tense and we drilled until dark. After dark, Captain Chester wanted us to be ready. He was a stickler for being prepared. Long after retiring, Captain Chester always bragged that he had never lost a man on any ship he had commanded. This was a record he was proud of.

Thursday—November 23, 1944
Today was the first action we had seen since leaving the States. While en route to Leyte at 1828 hours, our convoy suddenly came under attack by six Japanese torpedo bombers (nicknamed "Jills"). One plane was shot down by our convoy, crashing into the sea about 250 yards astern of the Cofer. The other planes hurried off afterwards.

Friday—November 24, 1944
Early in the day, unidentified planes kept showing up on the radar, but all were out of range. Some could have been Japanese bombers and some friendly, but until they got close enough to be identified by the IFF beacon, you could never be sure. The IFF, or "Identification, Friend or Foe," was used to identify friendly targets. However, if the suspicious plane did not communicate with the IFF interrogation, it was uncertain whether it was friendly or foe. This meant that we had to be prepared for each plane picked up on radar as if it was the enemy.

At 1255 hours, we arrived and anchored in the Pedra Harbor in Leyte. This was to be our homeport for our time in the South Pacific. At 1429 hours, a Jap fighter dropped a bomb on the PS-1124, which was moored alongside the AO-61. A minute later, the Cofer opened fire on the Jap fighters off our port side. Those same bombers were later seen trailing smoke and losing altitude.

Saturday—November 25, 1944
Our convoy left Leyte escorting a group of LST (Landing Ship, Tank) ships to Palau, Caroline Islands at speeds of 9 knots. At 0533 hours, radar contact was made with another Jap plane. It circled and then left. We continued screening our convoy at 9 knots; sometime up to 10 knots.

Sunday—November 26, 1944
Steaming with the sister ships in our Division #103: the USS Liddle (APD-60), USS Kephart (APD-61), USS Lloyd (APD-63), plus five other ships—mostly Destroyer Escorts.

Monday—November 27, 1944
Today the Cofer increased speeds to 18 knots. We took on fuel from the tanker USS Savgatuck (AO-75).

Tuesday—November 28, 1944
The Cofer left Palau to return back to Leyte. Our gun crews made daily exercises of pointer and trainer drills throughout the day.

Wednesday—November 29, 1944
Today the Cofer anchored in San Pedro Bay, Leyte and then went to General Quarters expecting a probable air attack.

At 1930 hours today, our starboard LCVP Boat number three's davit was rendered inoperative due to someone not pulling a pin before running it through the davit. The davit is a 7 ½ ton steel beam that was used to load the LCVP boats aboard the Cofer. (Later this davit broke, killing one man and badly injuring another. This was not the LCVP that I was assigned to.)

Thursday—November 30, 1944
We spent the day under "Flash Red" conditions and were put on General Quarters several times, expecting probable air attacks.

Friday—December 1, 1944
The Cofer began preparations to embark troops from the US Army #77 Division to the Ormac Bay at Leyte. At 2016 hours, a submarine was reported 27 miles from our anchored position and all watches were double alerted.

Monday—December 4, 1944
A board of investigation headed by Lieutenant Charles H. Cofer met to inquire into the davit cable trouble on November 29th. Lt. Cofer was the Executive Officer of the USS Cofer.

Tuesday—December 5, 1944
Today the Cofer remained at anchor in the San Pedro Bay maintaining war-cruising conditions while making preparations to get underway to rendezvous with other units from our Division #103.

Wednesday—December 6, 1944
At 0615 hours, we began preparations for our first invasion. By 0935 hours, the Cofer received 7 officers and 129 enlisted men from the 307th regiment, 77th Division of the 24th U.S. Army. These troops were planning a landing on the Rizaz Beach in Ormac Bay on the Island of Leyte. The Cofer got underway at 1230 hours for Ormac Bay.

Thursday—December 7, 1944
(Anniversary of Pearl Harbor Day—three years later)
We were steaming at 8 and then 7 knots toward Ormac Bay, arriving at 0625 hours. Our 4 LCVP boats were to disembark the troops for a second wave landing on White Beach #1. Twenty-two minutes later, all four boats were loaded with troops and clear of the Cofer, proceeding to the line of departure to hit our target beach.

It took about one hour and ten minutes for our four boats to hit the beach, unload the troops, and return to the Cofer. Once the LCVP boats were hoisted aboard, the Cofer would return to her screening duties.

At 0830 hours, several unidentified landing barges were sighted six miles away. The Cofer was sent to investigate but was called back due to the probability of enemy minefields in the target area. Meanwhile, all hell broke loose when enemy aircraft engaged our air cover, diving toward our ship. We opened fire on a Jap "Zero," which in turn dove at the USS Liddle (APD-60) at 1123 hours. The Zero was shot down two minutes later off the stern of the USS Liddle by our Cofer 5-inch gun.

At approximately the same time, the USS Mahan (DD-34) and the USS Ward (APD-16) were sunk from enemy suicide bomber attacks. (Note: The Ward was originally built as an old four-stack World War I Destroyer and was then converted to an APD. She was the first ship to fire a shot at the enemy at Pearl Harbor. She sank a Japanese two-man sub just hours before the Japanese bombed Pearl Harbor. She is now lost at the bottom of Ormac Bay.)

Minutes later, a second Zero made a suicide dive straight into the Liddle. The Cofer's guns were unable to fire at this plane because of the location of the USS Liddle, which left the plane open to crash into the bridge section of the Liddle.

In the thick of the battle, the Cofer hurried to offer assistance to the Liddle that was sailing in circles. It was clear that she had sustained substantial damage from the suicide bomber. Our division commander, Admiral Parson, wanted the Cofer to sink the Liddle because she was obviously rendered unsalvable. But, our Captain Chester pleaded with Admiral Parson for a chance to save her. After the Admiral agreed, a message was sent over to standby, informing the Liddle that we would be taking survivors. When no answer was received, Captain Chester called over to the Liddle using a bullhorn to ask who was in charge. When a sailor yelled back, "Nobody. They're all dead," we knew it was bad. Because of the direct hit to the bridge section, all Liddle communication and radar had been destroyed.

Captain Chester sent one of our LCVP boats and five of our crew members over to render assistance to the Liddle as needed including Coxswain Scaffide; Dr. Harold L. Wendelken, M.C. USNR; Warton, M.D. USNR; a signalman (whose name I will not mention); and J.S. Cleland D, USNR. The signalman who originally went to assist the Liddle begged to be sent back to the Cofer because he couldn't handle the carnage aboard the damaged ship. Art Conn, Signalman, 2nd Class, and I later volunteered to go over to serve as signalmen.

When arriving aboard the Liddle, it was like we had entered a scene from hell. Body parts were everywhere, some burned to the deck. Art Conn and I worked all night relaying signals, treating the wounded, and taking care of the dead. With men from the Cofer, the surviving crew slowly got the steering under manual control and saved the ship.

All in all, 38 out of the 225 men aboard the Liddle were killed on and more than 100 were injured. The majority of these casualties were officers who had been on the bridge where the suicide plane had hit. The Japanese suicide planes always tried to hit a ship's bridge because that's where the top officers were located. On this day, all of the Liddle's officers, including the ship's doctor, were on the bridge watching what was going on during the air attack. Only five officers survived—one of which had been blown off the bridge from the impact of the blast and into the ocean.

At 1315 hours, the Cofer took on board two extra LCVP boats from the USS Liddle. At 1325 hours, the Cofer proceeded to station an inner screen on the starboard beam of the convoy while en route to San Pedro Bay off of Leyte Island.

While the five of us Cofer men were assisting the Liddle at 1430 hours, more enemy planes dove at the USS Lamson (DD-36T), crashing into the after part of her deckhouse, sweeping forward through the after funnel, and enclosing the ship in flames. A rescue tug was sent to assist, extinguishing fire and taking the damaged ship in tow. Ten minutes later, the Cofer began firing at an enemy plane, type "Dinah," off the starboard beam. A combined task force shot down the plane. At 1500 hours the Cofer opened fire again on an enemy plane, type "Zeke," off the port side and by 1528 hours it was knocked down by the Cofer, falling off our port side.

At 1549 hours, another enemy plane was shot down in flames off our starboard bow by the P-38. After all was done, we lost four ships due to enemy action—the USS Liddle (APD-60), the USS Mahan (DD-364), USS Ward (APD-16) and USS Lamson.

Thursday—December 7, 1944

Art Conn and I rode the damaged USS Liddle back from Ormac Bay to San Pedro Bay, arriving about 0900 hours on December 8th. Because the bridge had been destroyed, the Liddle had to be steered from the aft steering below deck. Art Conn and I, along with other volunteers, continued to work through the early morning hours. It was raining and all I can remember is that there was so much blood everywhere. When we walked through the crew quarters below deck, sloshing through the trapped water made me feel like I was wading through a pool of blood. While below deck, I picked up a picture floating in the water that was a photo of the Liddle's crew from up above.

At daylight, I volunteered with several other men to scoop up body parts from what had been the bridge section of the Liddle. Like I mentioned earlier, body parts were everywhere, some even burned to the deck. (Both Conn and I later received a bronze star for displaying "courageous and prompt actions, unrelenting perseverance, and steadfast devotion to duty.") Conn and I returned to the Cofer at 10:00 a.m. after having spent about 22 hours aboard the USS Liddle. The Liddle was then towed back to the States for repairs and later saw action in Korea during the Korean War.

I should note that on this day, my Uncle's brother was also killed in the 77th Infantry at Ormac Bay. His name was Horward Conway. My wife and I later attended his funeral many years later when his body was returned to his hometown of East View, Kentucky.

Saturday—December 9, 1944
The Cofer remained anchored in San Pedro Bay, maintaining war-cruising conditions. No action today—to our great relief.

Monday—December 11, 1944
We traveled to Vicia Point in San Pedro Bay in Leyte to load troops. We picked up 131 enlisted men and 6 officers from the 19th Infantry-Regiment of the 24th Army Division for another planned invasion off Mindora Island.

While our LCVP boats brought ammunition aboard, one of our boat engineers, Arlo Kolthoff, was injured due to a fall from a rope ladder. When he fell, he landed on a GI's M-1 rifle which went up his rectum. (He later lived a full life, but never overcame this injury. He passed away in 1997.)

We left Leyte for Mindora at 1440 hours with our three sister ships in the Com.DIV.103: the USS Newman (APD-59), USS Kephart (APD-61), and the USS Lloyd (APD-63).

Wednesday—December 13, 1944
While traveling en route to our next invasion off the Mindora Islands, the Cofer traveled with the USS Nashville (CL-43) at 8.5 knots. In the afternoon, there we several dogfights near our convoy. At 1457 hours, I personally saw the Nashville get hit by a Jap suicide plane. During this fight, three Jap "Lilly" bombers and one Jap "Dinah" bomber were shot down by our convoy. I remember seeing two American P-38 ships firing at one Jap plane and we could hear the American pilots talking over the radio. One pilot yelled, "We got him!" I saw a splash, but the Japanese plane somehow kept flying. They finished him off with the next round.

These suicide planes were usually piloted by young boys who had just enough experience to get the plane off the ground and fly it into something. But I must say, the Japanese were the greatest fighters I have ever seen. They believed in dying for their country—refusing to surrender and fighting to the end.

Thursday—December 14, 1944
Throughout the morning, the Japanese were bombing the YMS wooden minesweepers that were ahead of our landing force. These YMS ships were 136-foot long wooden coastal sweepers that cleared the mine-infested seas for the Allied convoys. They were made of wood so they wouldn't set off magnetic mines.

One Jap plane was shot down at 1330 hours and luckily there were no causalities on the YMS minesweepers. Enemy aircraft kept approaching the landing force convoy at 1757 hours, but they kept their distance.

Friday—December 15, 1944
At 0525 hours, our screening destroyers sunk a surface-type craft. An hour later, we loaded troops into our four LCVP boats and landed them as part of a second wave to hit White Beach on the Mindora Islands—our LCVP boats' second invasion.

At 0802 hours our boats were hoisted back aboard the Cofer as American fighters shot down more enemy planes. Approximately 11 enemy planes believed to be "Kate" type attacked just off our landing beaches. The Cofer shot down one of those planes while two other planes dove at two LST boats landing on the beach. Our fighters shot down another one of those planes and only one plane of the 11 got away. As always, after we dispatched the troops, the Cofer returned to screening the convoy. At 1815 hours, all was clear of enemy planes and an hour later we increased our speed to 11 knots.

Saturday—December 16, 1944
Our convoy left Mindora and headed back to San Pedro Bay at Leyte. While en route, we had to rush to General Quarters several times as unidentified planes approached. At 1648 hours, one enemy plane was sighted and American fighters shot it down five minutes later.

Sunday—December 17, 1944
We arrived in Leyte at 0948 hours.

Monday—December 18, 1944
Remained anchored in Leyte maintaining war-cruising watch.

Today was a big change for our ship. At 1330 hours, our Captain, Alvin P. Chester, D.M. USNR, transferred for medical reasons to the USS Hope (AH-7). Lieutenant Herbert C. McClees, D. USNR relieved Captain Chester and Lieutenant C.H. Cofer, D. USNR assumed duties as Executive Officer of the Cofer.

Tuesday—December 19, 1944
Still anchored in San Pedro Bay. Today was the first day that I can remember that a captain's mast was held aboard our ship. 50 to 100 hours of extra duty were awarded to nine enlisted men for standing improper watch. The Captain insisted on each officer and man doing his part, and then some. So when someone failed to stand watch properly, the captain was tough—and he was respected tremendously for this. As he would say, failing to do your part could cost many lives or account for the loss of the ship. So, if you were on watch, you had better be alert and fulfill your responsibilities or else you would answer to the captain!

Wednesday—December 20, 1944
Today the Cofer remained anchored and received 26 sailors aboard to accompany us to Hollandia, New Guinea. We left for New Guinea at 1062 hours streaming at 15 knots with our sister ships.

Friday—December 22, 1944
Still en route to Hollandia, New Guinea at 15 knot speeds. As always, going to our battle station watches today before sunrise and again before sunset.

Sunday—December 24, 1944
We arrived on Hamadi Island in Humboldt Bay, New Guinea at 0948 hours. A number of men transferred to the USS Blue Ridge (AG-62).

Monday—December 25, 1944
Each day when not on watch, even though it was Christmas Day, was spent chipping paint, applying a yellow coronate, and then another coat of grey for the finish on the ship's deck. The salt water wrecked havoc on our ship and continuously needed maintenance.

Wednesday—December 27, 1944
Some men transferred from the Cofer, some onto the Cofer.

Thursday—December 28, 1944
Our LVCP boat #3 sustained another casualty to the starboard davit winch. This is the same davit that had been damaged on November 29th. Repairs were requested because the pinion and ring gears were stripped.

Friday—December 29, 1944
Davit repairs were completed and we left Hollandia for Noemfoor Island. At 1000

hours, the Cofer was instructed to search for a downed plane and its survivors—sadly none were found.

Saturday—December 30, 1944
The Cofer arrived and anchored for the next few days off Noemfoor Island, New Guinea.

Monday—January 1, 1945
At Noemfoor Island we took on 5 officers and 128 enlisted men to take to Luzon Island for our third Philippine invasion. We set sail traveling at 22 knots with our sister ships of the Division #103 at 0805 hours. While en route, our engines were stopped due to excessive vibrations. Divers were sent overboard to inspect the ship's screws. One propeller blade had a chip ¼ inch wide and 6 inches long. It was decided that this was not a problem, but speeds were reduced to 20 knots. The ship received oil and we set off to Luzon Island.

Tuesday—January 2, 1945
As we were cruising toward Luzon Island, extreme vibrations were again noticed on the Cofer. Our ship cut speeds and when no further vibrations were noticed, we resumed speeds at 17 knots. We later joined a fleet of big troop transports: the USS Leon (APA-48), USS Adaib (APA-91), USS Haskell (APA-117), and the USS Diphdia (AKA-59) and reduced speeds to 9 knots. We all went through a simulated landing and a mock shore bombardment. An Australian P-40 came over to help simulate diving and strafing our landing force. (Strafing is the term used for target practice from a target towed by a flying airplane.) Those Australian pilots were daredevils—coming, what seemed to us, too close before pulling out of their dives.

At 1130 hours, we were ordered to start laying a smoke screen. We did this often, intending to hide our convoy from the enemy—especially enemy aircraft. Between noon and 1400 hours, all troops had returned to our ship from their drills and by 1526 hours we were underway, headed for Noemfoor Island. As usual, the Cofer was in the screening position in front of the larger transport ships.

Wednesday—January 3, 1945
Still headed for Noemfoor Island. At 2130 hours the boilers were lit off as we headed for the entrance of the harbor doing anti-submarine patrol three miles offshore.

Thursday—January 4, 1945
Our convoy spent the full day doing anti-submarine patrol, cruising at the harbor entrance at 11 knots.

Friday—January 5, 1945
In the morning, we increased patrolling speeds to 14 knots. The Cofer left her patrolling post and joined other ships while awaiting a balance of our convoy. When all joined together, our speeds were set at 13 knots for Lingayen Gulf.

Left: Edwin J. McClendon, my LCVP boat division's officer and a long time personal friend.

Bottom Left: Art Conn, Signalman, 2nd Class who volunteered with me to assist the USS Liddle when it was hit by a suicide plane.

Bottom Right: Me aboard ship with my signalman's flags.

My Ordinance Division (left to right) Top row: J. Snellen, I. Fouts, M. Glozer.
Middle row—T. Ball, D. Mericle, E. Przybyl, Floyd. Bottom row—Dickerson, H.S.
Parrish, A. Sherrwood, and G. Elmore.
Bottom: Joe Wajerski, Quartermaster, 3rd Class from our LCVP boat #3
with myself on the right.

USS Cofer (APD-62)

5

Saturday—January 6, 1945
The entire convoy headed, as directed, for the biggest invasion as of yet in the South Pacific—Lingayen Gulf off of Luzon Island. By now, more than a hundred ships had joined in the convoy. Our speeds were still only 13 knots. As mentioned before, our ship could go double this speed, but the LCI and LST ships in our convoy could not. These slower speeds made our ship a sitting duck for the Jap submarines and planes.

Sunday—January 7, 1945
All day we continued streaming toward the Lingayen Gulf, Philippine Islands, cruising at 13.5 knots. Several times General Quarters was sounded, but so far, the planes that our radar had identified had been friendly.

The destroyer USS Norman Scott (DD-690) detected underwater sounds and dropped depth charges, but no submarine was confirmed.

Monday—January 8, 1945
En route to Lingayen Gulf. The Cofer was cruising with hundreds of ships at 9 knots, now doing the usual screening work and zigzagging duties. At 2342 hours we increased speeds to 12 knots and laid a smoke screen for the convoy.

Tuesday—January 9, 1945
Still cruising toward Lingayen Gulf at Luzon Island, Philippines at an average speed of 10.5 knots.

Wednesday—January 10, 1945
Cruising toward Lingayen Gulf, the Cofer was mostly zigzagging and laying a smoke screen to help hide our ships.

Finally at 0843 hours, our two davits (one on each side of the Cofer) put our four LCVP boats in the water and we loaded the troops that had been aboard since January 1st.

Even though they were headed for battle to take on the Japanese forces at Luzon Island, many of these GIs (the nickname we used for Army men) were pleased to get off our ship. Most GIs disliked traveling at sea and many got seasick. Most Army men preferred wet fox holes to Navy life, but all appreciated our food aboard ship, which to us was horrible! To them, anything was better than their Army "C" rations known as "hard tack." Our food was mostly Spam fixed different ways with dehydrated potatoes. Sometimes we would get "lamb" meat from Australia or New Zealand, which we called goat. This was our only fresh meat while in the South Pacific. To this day, I am different from most World War II veterans; I still love to eat Spam!

The four Attack Personnel Destroyers in our division (being one short of our original five since the Liddle's destruction) were always the first ships to hit the beaches. The APD ships were fast and we could quickly unload our LCVP boats to put the initial troops ashore. If all four sister ships were involved, we could land approximately 540 troops. After landing our initial troops, the larger ships put their troops ashore, including APAs (Attack Transports), AKAs (Attack Cargo Ships), the LCI (Landing Craft Infantry), and the LST ships (Landing Ship Tanks).

Lingayen turned out to be the biggest Pacific invasion yet. Once lowered into the water, our LCVP boats circled the Cofer and headed for the beach to put ashore the 135 troops and officers.

Thursday—January 11, 1945
There were still many, many ships (both US Navy and merchant ships) traveling in our convoy. Today the larger ships and LST ships spent the day unloading more troops ashore. For the Cofer, other than being on edge, nothing of importance was reported.

Friday—January 12, 1945
While in Lingayen Gulf, all started happening today. At 0640 hours, a Japanese suicide plane crash-dove into the USS Gilligan (DE-508). At 0710 hours another enemy plane crashed into the USS Richard W. Seusens (DE-342). Both enemy planes were out of range of our ship's guns.

At 0800 hours, enemy planes were sighted off our port side and three minutes later, enemy planes crash-dove into the USS Belknap (APD-34). By this time, our ship had done so much firing that we were concerned about having an ammunition shortage. The Cofer was then assigned to screen the harbor entrance area, which made us a sitting duck for Japanese suicide planes.

Saturday—January 13, 1945
Early this morning we received orders to proceed to our home base at Tacloban, Leyte Island. At 0821 hours, an enemy plane dove out of clouds and the Cofer opened fire with all her guns would bear, but the plane managed to dive into the USS Zelin (APA-3). We then started zigzagging and did so until 1940 hours.

Sunday—January 14, 1945
Uneventful day, doing usual on-deck duties while en route to our homeport of Tacloban, Leyte.

Monday—January 15, 1945
Same as yesterday. We picked up a suspected submarine radar contact, but later the contact was lost.

Tuesday—January 16, 1945
At 1742 hours, we finally dropped anchor in our homeport of Leyte Gulf—this was almost like a day of rest for us.

Wednesday—January 17, 1945
By mid-afternoon, we were making preparations for getting underway soon. We took on our usual amount of fuel of around 34,000 gallons.

Thursday—January 18, 1945
Still anchored at Tacloban, yet on standby to get underway at a few minute's notice. To our surprise, we remained in the same position for five more days.

Wednesday—January 24, 1945
We finally moved to Virginia Point, Leyte off Samar Island. Since conditions were normal, it was a good time to hold a captain's mast. Two sailors were punished to serve 25 hours of extra duty for reading a book while on watch.

Thursday—January 25, 1945
Still anchored at Virginia Point, Leyte.

Friday—January 26, 1945
At 0955 hours, we finally got underway en route to Luzon. We did screening for the convoy consisting of our APD sister ships: the USS Picking (DD-685), the USS Harris (APA-2) and the USS Mount McKinley (AGC-7). At 1415 hours, our convoy was joined by the Hmas Warresto (U-73), cruising at 11 knots.

Saturday—January 27, 1945
Early this morning we started zigzagging and continued doing so until 1150 hours. All the while, unidentified planes would show up on the radar as far away as 40 miles and we would be called to General Quarters until they were identified. At 2132 hours, we ceased zigzagging.

Sunday—January 28, 1945
Still cruising and zigzagging as the Screen Commander deemed necessary. We increased our speeds to 12 knots en route to Luzon.

Monday—January 29, 1945
As we got underway today, something happened that I believe later contributed to a disaster. The Cofer's cable on the starboard davit holding LCVP boat #3 parted yet again. This is the same davit that was damaged a few weeks ago. Our crew quickly began repairs. Meanwhile, we took one LCM in tow. This was also the first time any YMS wooden minesweeping boats had joined us, including the YMS-398, 334, 71 and 68.

Finally, our convoy reached Danto Nino on Luzon Island. There were many British and Australian ships amongst the group of ships finally arriving and anchored with ours.

Tuesday—January 30, 1945
We were headed for San Narcisco, Philippine Islands, and then to Grande Island in the Subic Bay for our fourth planned landing of troops from the 38th Infantry.

This turned out to be an easy landing; the boat crews landed our troops and got out of the way. As we were pulling off the beach, I remember seeing an old, damaged American 16-inch gun sitting on the beach, pointed out at us. It was certainly a funny feeling heading out in those tiny little LCVP boats and seeing that big gun pointed at you.

Our four LCVP boats were hoisted back aboard at 1300 hours and we were again underway by 1510 hours at 15 knots. By 1600 hours, the Cofer returned to screening the convoy as we headed back to Leyte with the Destroyer USS (DD-657). Four patrol craft joined us to screen for a group of LST ships, which meant we could only cruise at 8 knots.

Wednesday—January 31, 1945
Still patrolling and screening the slow moving convoy en route back to Leyte.

Thursday & Friday—February 1 and 2, 1945
We were still heading back to Leyte, traveling at a slow 9 knots. A possible enemy submarine was reported at 0835 hours, but nothing confirmed.

Saturday—February 3, 1945
En route to Leyte and cruising at 9 knots, finally arriving at Leyte at 0950 hours.

Sunday—February 4, 1945
Anchored in Leyte. During our stay here, a few of us were allowed to go ashore. There, we were each given two cans of beer because it was against Navy rules to drink aboard ship. (I would usually give mine to other sailors.) Another exciting thing about being in our home port is that we were able to show movies on the fantail of our ship. A screen would be set up and we were able to watch some pretty good movies! When finished with a movie, we would trade the other ships for their movies.

Monday & Tuesday—February 5 and 6, 1945
Remained at anchor in Leyte.

Wednesday—February 7, 1945
While on patrol, our LCVP boat #1 accidentally collided with two Filipino men in an outrigger canoe. The men were brought aboard and luckily, no injuries were found. We furnished them with a change of clothes, food, and our ship's experts repaired their canoe. The Filipino men seemed most pleased with our "help."

Thursday—February 8, 1945
Still anchored in Leyte. We enjoyed this because we could travel daily to the post office in Tacloban, Leyte in hopes of receiving mail. Sometimes it would be weeks before our mail would catch up with us at sea. When mail was finally received aboard ship, P.J. Adams, our mailman, would call out our names to hand out the mail. Nothing was more exciting than hearing your name called by P.J. Adams!

Friday—February 9, 1945
The Cofer got underway again at 0630 hours, but only to move to another section of the Leyte harbor. Then we anchored again.

Saturday—February 10, 1945
Only activity today was to take on 2,700 gallons of fuel. We received orders to prepare to travel to Subic Bay.

Tuesday—February 13, 1945
At 0830 hours, we got underway and also picked up our mail. By 1215 hours, we stopped again to pick up a few officers and men of the "RAN" (Royal Australian Navy) to take them to Subic Bay, Philippine Islands. The Cofer was ordered to once again take up a screening position for the convoy. We traveled at 17 knots—but the convoy, which included many merchant ships, traveled at an extremely slow pace of 5 knots.

Wednesday—February 14, 1945
We picked up mail from the SC-698 with orders to deliver it to the various ships in our convoy. Most of the day was spent exercising drills for the gun crew, depth charge settings, rescuing survivors, and boat drills.

    Note: One of my responsibilities was to set the depth charges. During a submarine hunt, I had to first put the required detonator inside the depth charges before they could be used. These were red, measuring about 4-inches long and about the size of a pencil in diameter and had to be handled with great care.

Thursday—February 15, 1945
Still cruising at the slow speed of 8 knots assisting the USS Thatcher (DD-514) with screening duties. All the while, we practiced smoke screening, gun drills, etc. Between 1638 and 1730 hours, we assisted in investigating a possible submarine contact. All was finally secured at 1930 hours with no official sub contact. Speeds were now down to 7 knots.

Friday—February 16, 1945
Still screening with the USS Thatcher (DD-514), escorting sections of Army, Navy and merchant ships. The Subic Bay group left our convoy at 1900 hours.

Saturday—February 17, 1945
En route to Subic Bay, escorting merchant ships, LST (Landing Ship, Tank) and LCT (Landing Craft Tank) ships at a slow speed of 6 knots. The other ships left us as we were assigned to escort the slow moving LCT ships to Subic Bay. The Cofer finally anchored at 1536 hours and took on a number of naval officers and men as passengers to be reassigned.

Sunday—February 18, 1945
Remained anchored at Subic Bay.

Monday—February 18, 1945
Today we took on 34,047 gallons of fuel oil.

Tuesday—February 19, 1945
Remained anchored with various units of Allied Naval and merchant ships.

Wednesday—February 20, 1945
No activity today.

Thursday—February 21, 1945
The Cofer was given the assignment to get underway for Mindora, Philippine Islands with the USS Lloyd (APD-63) in a zigzagging course at 16 knots. We reduced speeds briefly to 12 knots due to a casualty aboard the USS Newman (APD-59). At 2025 hours, we increased speeds again to zigzag at 16 knots.

Friday—February 22, 1945
At 0815 hours, we left Subic Bay for Mindora, escorting several fast moving ships, mostly APD ships, and this time we were traveling at 16 knots. By noon we were anchored at Mangarin Bay in Mindoro.

Friday—February 23, 1945
Today we took aboard 92 Army officers and enlisted men from Company "B" of the 186th Infantry along with a Captain, three Lieutenants and a balance of enlisted men.

Saturday—February 24, 1945
We received 29 more of Company "B's" 186th Infantry Division troops. This brought the total Army troops up to 121, so each of our 4 LCVP boats would have 30 men to port ashore at our next landing.

At 1300 hours, two of our shipmates were called to captain's mast. One received 50 hours of extra duty, the other 100 hours.

Sunday—February 25, 1945
We lowered our 4 LCVP boats and, as usual, proceeded to the fantail to load all 121 Army troops of the 138th Infantry Division for a practice landing on Mindora Island. It took us seven minutes to get all 121 troops aboard our four landing craft. Then our boats traveled as fast as we could to the rendezvous area. We all circled the area until the final word was given and then we headed for the beach. (In all of our time in the South Pacific, our four boats were never assigned to be

part of the first wave to hit the beach. As I remember, we were always in the second or third wave to hit the beach.) By 0930 hours, we had made the practice landing, taken the same troops back to the Cofer, unloaded them, and then hoisted our four boats aboard the Cofer.

Monday–February 26, 1945
Today we took aboard a special Navy Lieutenant for temporary duty. This afternoon we left Mindora for our sixth invasion with the 186th Infantry.

At 1730 hours, we set sail from Mindora and, as usual, we had no idea where we were headed. This would be our sixth invasion. When preparing for upcoming invasions, our group of four APD ships traveled together, accompanied this time by the USS Rushmore (LSD-14) landing ship dock.

Tuesday–February 27, 1945
Today we finally learned that we were headed for Puerto Princesa at Palawan in the Philippine Islands, just north of Borneo.

Also in this invasion convoy were four YMS wooden minesweepers, the YMS-52, 71, 340 and the 481. (The 481 was later sunk at Tarakan, Borneo).

Wednesday–February 28, 1945
We arrived at Puerto Princesa Bay at 0817 hours. A minute after dropping anchor, we began loading the Army troops into our four landing craft. Seven minutes later our LCVP landing craft were clear of the Cofer, headed for the usual rendezvous. We made a circle of the ship and headed for the beaches. Very little enemy fire was encountered by the time we hit the beach and all 4 boats unloaded their boatloads of troops. At 0932 hours, we were back to the Cofer.

Unless at General Quarters, our LCVP boats would get to the edge of the Cofer as quick as possible and look toward the beach area to see what may be of interest. On this day, I particularly remember seeing a train coming around the hill on the left of the island. Suddenly, one of our ships opened up its guns, knocking the train right off the mountainside. Naturally we all applauded. But sadly at about the same time to our right, we saw a huge fire break out. We thought nothing of the fire because of the usual Japanese efforts to destroy everything they could to prevent the Allies from gaining an advantage. Later we were shocked to learn that the building was actually holding 400 or more Allied Prisoners of War (POWs). The Japanese had set the building on fire after the troops landed on the beach. Many years later, I read accounts of this building being burned, and according to the published story, it was absolutely horrible.

At 1800 hours, we pulled anchor and got underway at 10 knots escorting various YMS, LCI, LSM, and LSD—14 ships in all, headed back to Mangarin Bay at Mindora.

Thursday—March 1, 1945
Still headed toward Mindora, escorting the convoy. Along the way we were suddenly ordered to join up with the USS O'Bannon (DD-450) because of suspected submarine contact in the area. We increased speeds to 22 knots to search for a possible Jap submarine. The USS Newman (APD-59) dropped depth charges and the second depth charge made sound contact. Although additional depth charges were dropped, no official proof was made of a submarine's presence, as first suspected. At 0800 hours, a second possible sub contact was made, but we later returned to regular cruising speeds.

At 1740 hours, another alert was reported and again at 2144 hours when the USS Newman (APD-59) sighted a periscope and she rushed to ram it. She dropped depth charges, but later decided it was not a sub.

The Cofer continued searching for a possible submarine with nothing confirmed, yet there were strong indications that a Japanese sub was in the vicinity. We stayed at General Quarters for most of the night.

Friday—March 2, 1945
All were finally secured from General Quarters at 0711 hours the next day. We changed course at 1030 hours to investigate a suspicious object in the water and it turned out to be an unoccupied native canoe. At 1500 hours, the Cofer reduced speeds to 5 knots to allow the USS Newman (APD-59) to make mechanical repairs. Fifteen minutes later, repairs were made and we were able to increase speeds back to 22 knots. At 1945 hours, we arrived back at Mangarin Bay at Mindora, dropped anchor, and set regular port security and usual watches.

Saturday—March 3, 1945
Remained at anchor at Mindora.

Sunday—March 4, 1945
Today was spent doing our usual watches and chipping the deck to remove rust, applying yellow paint for a base, and the regular Navy grey on top. We never stopped chipping and painting when at anchor. At 1845 hours, 147 troop officers and enlisted men of the Company "L" of the 162nd Infantry, 41st Division came aboard.

Monday—March 5, 1945
At 0900 hours, all 147 Company "L" troops boarded our four LCVP landing crafts and we made a practice landing on Mindora. The trial run came off good. We left the troops ashore overnight.

Tuesday—March 6, 1945
At 1630 hours, our 4 boats picked up the 147 troops again off Mindora.

Wednesday—March 7, 1945
Today one of my shipmates, who later became a good friend, was awarded the most punishment I had seen yet. He was caught sleeping on watch. He received 10 days of solitary confinement on bread and water with full rations every third day and a loss of $15 pay for 2 months. I was thankfully never put on captain's mast during my entire time aboard the USS Cofer.

Thursday—March 8, 1945
At 0630 hours, the Cofer was off again. We had received orders to leave Mindoro with the troops to be landed in our seventh invasion at Zamboanga, Mindanao. As usual, with the slower ships in our convoy, we were cruising at only 8 knots and later at 5 knots. To me, this was like crawling. Just before midnight we did increase our speed to 6.5 knots, although this was still too slow for a ship that could cruise at 23 knots.

6

Friday—March 9, 1945
Still cruising between 6.5 and 8 knots toward our scheduled invasion island of Mindanao City on Zamboanga, in the Philippines. Zamboanga would be our seventh Philippine invasion. For the past few years, Zamboanga had been the headquarters for Philippine terrorists.

The troops we put ashore were instructed to hold the beach until the bigger forces could arrive. After hitting the beach, our Coxswain dropped the ramp for the troops to run ashore and I jumped forward to assist the engineer in cranking up the steel ramp as we backed off the enemy beach. When the steel ramp was down, he and I were exposed briefly to the enemy beach, so we worked hard to get the ramp back up as fast as possible. Then it was my responsibility to run forward and hook the two top catches of the steel ramp, one of each side, to lock them in place. I would usually crawl up on the ramp and stick my head over to see what I could on the beach as we were backing off.

On this morning, as I was trying to see what action was going on ashore, I kept hearing bullets zinging around me. I assumed that it was a LCI (Landing Craft, Infantry) in the background shooting over our heads. (This was normal for the LCI boats to do! Usually they would let go of hundreds of rounds of rockets just over our heads—which was really frightening, to say the least. They'd scare the tar out of you!) For some reason, I glanced toward the rear of our boat and realized that the bullets were splashing all around us at the back end of our boat. Recognizing the enemy fire, I quickly dropped back down in the boat.

Although our boat was not hit, Zamboanga had not been an easy invasion for us. We returned to the ship by 1120 hours and were hoisted aboard with no casualties.

Sunday—March 11, 1945
When finished at Zamboanga, we were ordered back to Mindora Island at 9.5 knots. As usual, we were performing our usual screening duties to help protect the convoy.

Monday—March 12, 1945
The Cofer arrived back at Mindora at 1455 hours, secured from special sea detail, and then started our usual anchor watch.

Tuesday—March 13, 1945
This morning boat #3's Gunner, Vinson Dehart, SI transferred off the Cofer to be returned to the States for discharge for being under age. If I remember correctly, he was only 15 years-old when entering the service and he had to be probably 16 at this time. I think it was his grandmother who alerted the Navy of his actual age.

Later this morning, we left to return to our home part of Tacloban, Leyte. As usual we zigzagged, escorting the convoy of ships headed for Leyte. At 0625 hours we were advised to investigate an unidentified object, which turned out to be a native sailing craft. We had been cruising at 20 knots but then reduced to 15 knots before preparing to anchor Leyte. After arriving back in Leyte we were able to take it easy for the next week.

Tuesday—March 20, 1945
At 1115 hours, the Captain held a captain's mast and three shipmates received penalties. I will not mention names, but all were for standing improper watch. One was a member of our boat crew and a good friend.

At 1730 hours, Arlo R. Kolthoff returned aboard for duty. After all these years, I had forgotten him reporting back aboard after his serious injury and recovery at the Navy Hospital San Francisco. (Earlier on December 11, 1944, while climbing down a rope ladder into his LCVP boat, he slipped and fell on a GI's M-1 rifle that went up his rectum—seriously injuring him.)

Wednesday—March 21, 1945
The Cofer got underway at 0758 hours, proceeding to Punubulu Island to pick up 120 officers and men from Company "L", 182nd Infantry Division. This included one Captain, two Lieutenants, one 1st Sergeant, six Staff Sergeants, and from other Army divisions: 1 Colonel, 1 Major, 2 more Captains, and 1 Lieutenant. At 1710 hours, our LCVP boats proceeded to Hinunangan Bay, Leyte for landing rehearsal exercises for the 120 Army personnel.

Thursday—March 22, 1945
My same shipmate friend received another penalty of reduced rank for improper watch after corrections on March 20th.

At 1445 hours, two Navy Ensigns came aboard for the upcoming amphibious landing.

Friday—March 23, 1945

At 0715 hours, the Cofer got underway with the USS Lloyd (APD-63), USS Kephard (APD-61), and USS Newman (APD-59) to practice a landing with the troops. At 1250 hours, we put the troops ashore and were heading back to the Cofer to be hoisted aboard when the waters became rough all around us. I was trying to put the cable in the front hook located in the middle of the troop area of our boat and get the davit beam hooked into the boat connection, but our boat was bouncing up and down in the rough waters. The Cofer's Executive Officer, Charles Cofer, yelled down to me on a bullhorn to get it hooked up fast. His demand hit me the wrong way as I was wrestling as best I could with the hook. I screamed back to him, "If you can do a better job, then get down here yourself." Fortunately for me, he said nothing else and those in the boat know I could have been court martialed because enlisted men never talked back to their officers.

I never heard a word about my yelling back to Mr. Cofer. Possibly he realized that he had been wrong to press the issue—I could have been in serious trouble. Of all of the officers aboard, Lieutenant Cofer was the one most determined to hit the Japanese at every opportunity to avenge his brother's death. The Cofer was named after his brother, John Joseph Cofer, Seaman, 1st Class, who had been a Rangefinder aboard the USS Aaron Ward. He was mortally wounded at Guadalcanal on November 12, 1942 while manning his station. His last words were, "I can range no longer."

Seaman John Joseph Cofer was later awarded a Silver Star for his courageous devotion to duty. So, it was fitting that our Lt. Cofer aboard the USS Cofer received two Silver Stars. He was the only person aboard the Cofer to receive such a special high Navy award.

Saturday—March 24, 1945

We were still anchored in Hinunangan Bay at Leyte waiting for word to get underway for the next landing. Finally, the word came at 1653 hours to get underway to Talisay Point at Cebu City, Philippines.

Sunday—March 25, 1945

Still underway toward Cebu City, the Philippine's second largest city, traveling between midnight and 4 a.m. at slow speeds of 6-8 knots. While approaching the long beach just to the left of the city of Cebu, we received orders to land the landing forces. Within 8 minutes, all four of our LCVP boats were loaded with infantrymen and put away from the ship. We could do this quickly—rope ladders dropped from each side of the ship off the fan tail with two boats on the starboard side and two on the port side. Within minutes, 30-36 men were down the rope ladders into the first boat and then the second boat did the same. We would then head for the rendezvous area, all boats circling in a counter-clockwise position until the word was given to head for the beach.

The Japs would usually back off the beaches to avoid our battleships and destroyers with their big guns and the B-24, B-25, and B-26 planes that would attempt to "soften up" the beaches to knock out as much as possible before our troops arrived. When the first landing craft hit the beaches, the Japs would rush forward to meet the invading Allied troops. (Throughout the Philippines, eight invasions were made with US troops and occasional Australian observers. My LCVP boat that I was assigned to landed invading troops in all eight invasions.)

Well before our landing craft reached the beach area, we knew we were in for trouble. On our radio, I heard conversations that snipers were in the bell tower of a church just to the left of where we were scheduled to hit. All hell was coming from the beach—mortar fare, as I best remember. When we got within, what I am guessing, 75 feet of the beach, our boat hit a coral reef. Whitaker, our Coxswain, tried to get us moving again, but could not get our boat to go any farther. The officer who was among the enlisted men in our boat screamed at Whitaker to go further—not to drop them in the waist-deep water. Whitaker informed him that it was impossible, due to the coral reef. Whitaker advised Gilbert Crippen and me to drop the ramp to the water's level. The troops jumped into waist high water and started wading toward the beach.

All men left our boat except for one G.I., listed as PFC Conrad Wessel in our ship's log. We heard a shot hit the left side of our boat, and naturally we thought it came from the beach. We turned quickly to see that PFC Wessel had been injured. His left hand, except for the fingers and skin had been blown away. I was the first to get to him. Much to my surprise, I saw an empty cartridge lying at the bottom of our boat. PFC Wessel of Company "L", 182nd Division had put his left hand over his M-1 rifle and pulled the trigger, rather than go ashore to face the horrible counter-resistance being put up by the Japs. I gave him two shots of morphine before we got him back to our ship. The Cofer turned him over to the Army and I often wonder what ever happened to him after that.

Now comes the saddest part. The 34 enlisted men and one officer that we had put ashore had to trudge through the water the rest of the way because our boat was not able to reach the beach. As they reached the beach, a mortar hit the middle of the group and we could only watch from a distance as they were blown to bits. We have no idea how many were killed or how many were injured. Sadly for them, had it not been for the coral reef, (the only one we ever hit), those 30-

some men would have been safely ashore. It would have been our boat blown to bits instead of those thirty men.

After we got the injured GI back to the Cofer, our boat crew was instructed to go to other ships and haul troops and supplies to the beach. It seemed every time we would take troops ashore, we would have to move a little farther down the beach. It was a rough day. By noon, our boat was hoisted back aboard the Cofer. The Cofer and other ships in the landing force had also had a busy day, due to enemy planes and a Jap sub sighting. At 1645 hours, we received orders to proceed out of the Cebu City area with the entire convoy. Radar contacts kept us at our battle stations until around midnight, but we were relieved to have Cebu City behind us.

Tuesday—March 27, 1945
Just after midnight our sister ship, the USS Newman (APD-59), reported a surfaced Japanese submarine and all of the convoy rushed to General Quarters. Luckily this time it turned out to be the LST-830. At 0430 hours, the Newman again reported a sub contact by sonar.

Then at 2035 hours, we were ordered to investigate another radar contact that turned out to be a native outrigger canoe with Philippine occupants. Again at 2108 hours, the same type of contact was made and it, too, turned out to be native Philippinos. We were then secured from General Quarters, moving along at a slow speed of 8 knots because some of the amphibian ships could only do 8 knots.

Wednesday—March 28, 1945
Today was a repeat of yesterday. At 0445 hours, we were advised to investigate a radar contact and it also turned out to be Philippinos in an outrigger canoe. Later, we had some concern with the Cofer's #2 main engine. The engineering section was able to make the necessary repairs, permitting us to keep pace with the convoy returning from the Cebu City invasion back to Leyte Gulf.

Thursday—March 29, 1945
At 0455 hours, the Cofer arrived back in Tacloban, Leyte Gulf. It was like returning home to be back in our homeport of Tacloban. We looked forward to hopefully receiving some mail from home. One of our boats would take P.J. Adams, who we referred to as our "mailman," to pick up our bags of mail. At mail call, it was good getting your name called out to accept letters from home. My mother wrote to me regularly, as well as other family members and friends. I also had four girls who often wrote to me. Being eighteen years old, letters from girls

were special! One was a cute girl from my hometown of Louisville, Kentucky. Another was a pretty Italian girl who I met at Ozone Park in New York City, and the other was a pretty Southern girl from Meridan, Mississippi. Lastly, I often exchanged letters with a girl from Waco, Texas, who was the sister of one of my shipmates, Charles L. Teague. After discharge, I traveled to Waco to visit her. We were serious about getting married, but we both realized that we were not ready to settle down. Actually, she was the one to point this out and later, I saw the wisdom in her decision. Her brother was a real friend to me.

Friday—March 30, 1945
Today was a leisure work day in Tacloban harbor. As always, we were scraping and painting unless on watch, at General Quarters, or asleep.

Saturday—March 31, 1945
At 1715 hours, we got underway again headed back to Mindaro Island. It was nice to be cruising at 14 knots for a change. We screened the convoy by zigzagging.

Sunday—April 1, 1945
At 0552 today, we went to General Quarters to investigate a radar contact, which was later identified as a friendly native sailboat. We then returned to zigzagging. At 0955 hours we ceased zigzagging and resumed a base course.

Monday—April 2, 1945
This morning, radar contact once again failed to be an enemy vessel, and we returned to our convoy. At 0744 hours, the USS (PC-1131) came along our starboard side to pass an anchorage chart. An hour later, we dropped anchor in Margarin Bay, Mindora, but were soon on our way again for Subic Bay at a good speed of 16 knots.

At 1245 hours, we anchored in Subic Bay, Luzon, Philippines. A court martial for Seaman O.L. Brown was conducted by Lieutenant Charles H. Cofer. I often wondered what was decided by the court martial. Later Lt. Cofer met again to try another shipmate who is a good friend and will remain nameless, at court martial.

We remained at anchor throughout the night, always keeping one boiler set for auxiliary purposes, in case we were ordered to get underway quickly.

Today the Cofer received four sets of small minesweeping gear to be installed in our LCVP boats. This was a surprise to all of us aboard the Cofer—it was something nobody had ever heard of before. The LCVP landing crafts were now to become shallow water minesweepers in the waters of Borneo to assist the larger YMS minesweepers that could not go into the shallow waters between enemy boat docks. We would be minesweeping in preparation for the British and Dutch Navies' landing forces.

There were many different types of mines that were used during World War II. It has been estimated that a fourth of all World War II ships were lost due to mines. Hundreds of thousands of contact mines were randomly strewn into the sea by both the Axis and Allied powers. This type of mine ignited when a victim physically touched the mine, breaking a glass vial containing an acid trigger. They could easily be spread by the thousands by surface vessels, submarines, or parachuted from aircraft. Another type of mine that was used was the acoustic mine, which was activated by sound vibrations. A pressure mine was another that ignited by changes in water pressure as ships moved over it. Lastly, magnetic mines were also used. The sheer number of mines that were spread throughout the South Pacific created a need to test our LCVP boats to become mine sweepers.

Friday—April 6, 1945
We remained at anchor in Subic Bay throughout the day. We took on fuel at 0945 hours from the USS Kenwood (IX-179). It took about an hour to complete the fueling of 25,000 gallons of diesel fuel.

Saturday—April 7, 1945
At 1825 hours, we got underway for Leyte accompanied by the YMS-51, 53, 73, LSM-1 and SC-698. At 1940 hours, we reduced speeds to five knots because the YMS-73 had an engineering problem.

Sunday—April 8, 1945
As always, we went to man our battle stations one hour before sunrise and one hour before sunset as the Navy felt this was the time the Japanese preferred to hit.

Monday—April 9, 1945
Still en route to Leyte at speeds of 8 knots.

At 1100 hours, we went through our usual gunnery exercises by firing every anti-aircraft gun we had aboard. Due to the large number of Jap suicide planes that we had encountered, we borrowed every 30 and 50-caliber guns we could find from the Army and welded them onto the iron posts that supported the cable railings around the Cofer.

This afternoon, sentences were passed out for the two sailors who had earlier been court martialed. I will not mention their names, especially because one is a personal friend still today. He was sentenced to solitary confinement on bread and water for a period of 20 days with full rations every third day with a loss of $35.00 of his pay per month for a period of six months. The total lost of earnings would amount to $210.00.

At 1915 hours, we were called to General Quarters and went through gun drills again.

7

Tuesday—April 10

This morning we were still underway to Leyte Gulf escorting the previously mentioned ships. We were loaded with minesweeping gear for the YMS minesweepers and our own four LCVPs. The LCVPs were to be hooked up for minesweeping in the Tarakan harbor in Borneo. The Cofer and her convoy would lie well outside the harbor while our four small boats were sent into the harbor hooked up with minesweeping gear. I doubt anyone had ever heard of an LCVP planning to do minesweeping. Today it is doubtful that anyone would be foolish enough to attempt such a project because of how close we would go to the enemy beaches—even in between the enemy boat docks. But we did not question our orders when our time came at Tarakan, Borneo.

Wednesday—April 11, 1945

At 0830 hours, we arrived at Leyte Gulf and anchored off Talosa; finally anchoring at Punubulu Island off the southern tip of Samar Island.

Thursday—April 12, 1945

Still anchored as before. Many units of the Allied Navies and merchant ships were present.

Friday—April 13, 1945

Still anchored in San Pedra Bay, Leyte. At 1030 hours, the Captain held an unusual inspection of the ship. Later, he held a captain's mast for a seaman accused of being late to relieve his watch. He was punished 50 hours of extra duty. The Captain was the judge AND jury—he assigned sentences as he felt justified.

Sunday—April 15, 1945

Still anchored. We received orders to be prepared to get under way, keeping one boiler in use for auxiliary purposes. At 0730 hours, we cut the #1 and #2 main engines and set special sea detail.

By 0852 hours, we were underway from San Pedro Bay en route to Guivan on

Samar Island for loading supplies. This morning, as many mornings before, we tested our smoke screening. This was so important when under air attack—we would throw up smoke to cover the ship to avoid being seen by enemy aircraft or even Japanese submarines.

At 1206 hours Lt. J.M. Connell, who was a harbor pilot, came aboard to pilot the Cofer through the shallow waters near Samar Island.

Monday—April 16, 1945
Still anchored off Samar Island. At 1100 hours, another captain's mast was held for one of the ship's bakers for sleeping in. Another Navy pilot, Ensign R.H. Schairer, USNR then came aboard to pilot us out of the shallow water harbor. Two hours later he left the ship and we started for special sea detail, cruising at 15 knots. At 1650 hours, we anchored again at San Pedra Bay, Leyte.

Friday—April 20, 1945
Today was a dull day, still anchored in San Pedra Bay. Before the day was over, we took on six additional crewmembers that were to be permanently assigned shipmates.

Saturday—April 21, 1945
Something happened that was sad today. Chief Pacifico Doroja, USN turned up Absent without Official Leave, AWOL, after many years of service. He had been home on leave in his native Philippines. Apparently, he went home with intention to never return. He, no doubt, lost his Navy benefits and later retirement.

Today, Manuel Menendez reported aboard for duty, who later became a true friend and long time Cofer Association supporter.

Sunday—April 22, 1945
At 0810 hours, we got underway for Zamboanga, Mindanao with a mixed convoy of Army, Navy, and merchant ships—21 ships in all. The Cofer set war-cruising conditions as we checked magazines, smoke powder, etc. Conditions were normal, but we were moving at slow speeds zigzagging amongst the smaller ships.

There was an evening alert and then we secured to normal at 1933 hours while maintaining 9 knots.

Tuesday—April 24, 1945
Still cruising en route to Zamboanga at 7 knots. At 0710 hours, we reduced speeds to 5 knots, awaiting the boarding of an officer with anchorage instructions

for entering the Zamboanga harbor. Previously, we had been involved in the invasion of Zamboanga on March 10. On that day, our LCVP boats landed Army troops just to the left of the city of Zamboanga, and it had not been an easy invasion for us.

Wednesday—April 25, 1945

We began preparations for our next big assignment at Tarakan Island, Borneo. Our convoy started to rendezvous in preparation for our trip. We pulled out at 9 knots, escorting other ships. At 0810 hours, four suspicious rafts were sighted in the water and since the Cofer was the flag ship, the LCI-359, LCI-228, LCS-28, and the YMS-73 were sent to investigate.

At 0850 hours, these boats reported occupants of these rafts to be Japanese soldiers, and they attempted to take the Japanese prisoners. The Japs, under orders to surrender, started killing themselves with demolition charges. A total of 32 Japanese died on those rafts. At 0945 hours, the ships returned to our convoy and we increased our speed to 9.5 knots.

Friday—April 27, 1945

Cruising as before with the British HMAS Lachlan (K-364) heading for Tarakan, Borneo with speeds of 9 knots. The convoy then reduced to 5 knots as the LCI, LCS, and the YMS minesweepers were falling back while the YMS ships were preparing to start minesweeping the assigned areas.

At 1025 hours, all four of our LCVP boats were in the water. We were to mine sweep the harbor to prepare for an upcoming invasion. Today was our first ever experience in minesweeping, and it was fun. The Cofer sent us in four small landing craft into the Jap harbor while she and other ships in our convoy lay in wait outside of the harbor entrance, out of range of the Japanese shore batteries. The boats were rigged to do their first shallow water minesweeping duty. A three square foot metal contraption called a paravane was hooked to a cable and winch and pulled behind our boat. The cable would float out a certain distance from the boat, hoping to snag a shallow water mine. The boat would travel very, very slow because the minesweeping gear slowed the small boat considerably. We would go within 150 yards of the enemy beaches to find and explode shallow water mines.

We easily knew when we snagged a mine because the boat would literally stop in the water. The sweeper would follow the mine's cable back to a gadget which had sharp teeth on it. We would know that the cable had been cut even before we would see the mine because our boat would shoot forward and the mine would suddenly pop up to the surface of the water. That is when our fun would start. Each boat had two 30-caliber machine guns mounted at the back. We would reel in the minesweeping gear and open up on the metal mine. Each mine had prongs sticking out and when one of those prongs was hit, the mine would explode. This was fun—our reward for finding a mine.

By 1815 hours, all four small boats were hoisted back aboard the Cofer. Boat #1 with Joe Scaffide as the Coxswain, had exploded one mine. My boat, Walter Whitaker's boat #2, cut one mine, but we were unable to explode it.

Saturday—April 28, 1945

Early this morning, all of our four LCVP boats were in the water again and proceeding to mine sweep. When we arrived in sight of Tarakan Island, we could see black smoke like you would not believe. We later learned that these were oil tanks that the Japanese had set on fire when they saw our convoy coming.

I should mention that the Cofer served many purposes for our convoy. In addition to furnishing the smaller ships with fresh water, the Cofer was like the hospital ship for the other ships. Our doctor, H.W. Wednleken and his pharmacist, D.G. Taylor, were kept very busy during our three invasions of Borneo. The American ships were primarily involved in the three Borneo operations to do minesweeping for the British, Dutch, and Australians because Borneo had been a Dutch providence before the Japanese took it over for the oil.

Sunday—April 29, 1945

By 0900 hours, we were in the water to start today's minesweeping operations. Even though it was dangerous, we had fun in our boats locating mines and firing at them until they were exploded. Today we even swept right in between the boat docks. The Japanese soldiers were all over the island between the big oil tanks, but they had dug in so we could not see them. Occasionally, they would open up on our small boats. Someone guessed they were using 37-mm guns, but we did not know. All I mostly remember is that they were big shells, yet they never hit any of our four boats. We figured they were not actually trying to hit us because we were as close to them as the length of a football field. They probably didn't want to give away their position. The four little guys in our small boat weren't worth it.

When they shot at us, we would pull in our boat's minesweeping gear and head out into the middle of the harbor until they stopped firing at us. Again, we could never figure out why they did not hit us, or at least our boat. We always thought they must have felt sorry for us—four little boats sweeping along the beaches while the big ships stayed well out of the harbor. The Cofer had a 5-inch 38-caliber gun in front, as well as 3 twin 40-millimeter guns, three 20-millimeter guns, and a number of 50-caliber and 30-calibers welded on the guard rail post to protect the Cofer against Kamikaze planes.

Monday—April 30, 1945

General Quarters sounded several times this day on the Cofer while we were in the Tarakan Harbor. The Cofer supplied fresh water to several YMS minesweepers throughout the day. As our LCVP boats went out to mine sweep today, the YMS-481 accompanied us as our guide. As before, the Japanese shore batteries threw more than 20 large shells at our little boat, but they never hit us. Whitaker, our Coxswain, did a super job of whipping our boat from left to right to avoid their shells. The shells caused water to splash over our boat, so we knew that each miss was a close call.

Tuesday—May 1, 1945

Today was not an easy day to relax as enemy planes were continuously being picked up on radar. The Allied Navies began pushing the Japanese back at Borneo where they had been getting their oil supply. Up until now, the Japs had had Borneo all to themselves. We were their first threat in Borneo, so we expected a lot to be thrown at us. The Japanese Navy, except for submarines, was surprisingly non-existent. Yet, our people knew that the Japanese still had some planes hidden on Borneo.

Today as our boats were sweeping between the boat docks, the Japs suddenly opened up on our small minesweeping boats. We strongly felt that they were just trying to frighten us by not actually hitting our boats. The island is narrow, and they were on the harbor side, blasting all around us. There was no way that they could they have accidentally missed our LCVP boats dragging minesweeping gear and moving about 2 knots (at most).

When the Japanese started firing at us, our Boat Officer McClendon ordered us to pull out into the middle of the harbor. As the shore batteries were letting us have it, he directed me to use our ship-to-shore radio to call the Cofer (call-named "Goldone") and request permission for us (call-named "Idiot") to return to the ship. I'll never forget radioing the Cofer saying, "Goldone-Goldone, this is Idiot Two. Come in please." I requested permission to return to the ship because enemy gun fire was too much. I said whatever McClendon told me to say, and I will always remember the Captain or Commodore's, (whichever he was) response, "Negative, Idiot Two, make a closer sweep to the beach." I did not have to relay the message to my boat officer because the Commander's response was obvious from the big beads of sweat that had popped out across my face and forehead.

We headed back toward the beach and the Japs played with us a little more, but they still did not hit any of our boats. They could have easily picked us off one by one with small-arms rifles. To this day, it's still a big mystery why they just played with us.

Finally finished, we started pulling in our minesweeping gear and headed back to the Cofer. Suddenly, the water broke half-way across the harbor and to our surprise, the bow of a two-man submarine broke the water. No periscope, just the bow and dome. Our four boats circled the submarine from left to right, firing on the dome with our 30-caliber machine guns. The bullets popped off, not hurting the dome in anyway. Someone yelled, "Let's ram it." But before we could do that, it submerged. McClendon yelled to me, "Call the Cofer."

I did, saying that a Jap sub had partially surfaced in front of us and we were firing on it. The Admiral fired back at me, "That's no sub, it's a fish."

I screamed back, "Fish my ass. I never saw a fish with rivets in it!"

The sub re-submerged into the harbor and got away—all because of that "KJapanese now-it-all" Admiral.

Boy was I in for it after that! When we arrived back at the Cofer, two guys were waiting for me and they practically dragged me up in front of the Admiral. Did he ever dress me down! McClendon, my boat officer, just stood behind me saying, "Yes, sir...yes, sir..."

The Admiral said, "I'm not going to court martial you this time. But Sailor, you don't use language like that on an Armed Forces radio." I will never forget those words.

Wednesday—May 2, 1945

The next day was even worse than yesterday. In fact, it was horrible. All ships proceeded around Tarakan Island to the north side called the Seajap Strait. Our boat, #2, was chosen to sweep a small channel before any of the larger ships could enter. Our little boat swept the channel and no mines were located. Again, we were never fired upon. The Japs were too smart to open up on four guys in a small boat when larger ships were waiting further out in the channel. We were at most within 50 feet of those large, probably 5-inch Japanese guns. When returning to the Cofer, for some reason, our boat was not hoisted aboard, and we cruised along the YMS-481, our lead ship, about 30 feet from her starboard side.

Unbeknownst to our small boat, however, two Tarakan natives had earlier warned our fleet that the Japanese had guns laid out on the point of the straight we were heading towards. When the YMS-481 got even with the channel point, those Japanese guns opened up. The first shot hit the magazine section of the YMS-481 and she exploded. With all of the ammunition that she had aboard, that wooden ship exploded and debris flew all over us in our boat. Whitaker, our Coxswain, took off for the middle of the small harbor as the Japanese fired at us— we guessed 25 large shells or more. Whitaker would flip the boat from one way and then to the other in the harbor and fortunately, not one shot hit our boat.

Unfortunately, we were unable to return to the Cofer through the main channel because all was ablaze. We found another small river that led into Tarakan's big harbor where we had mine swept earlier. The Cofer, with her 5-inch 38 guns, came blazing toward the point where the big shore batteries were. I can vividly remember seeing the phosphorus shells that were thrown at the Japanese from our ships. The exploding shells were like five fingers widespread in the air. I can still hear those Japs scream as the phosphorus did its job, burning the skin down to the bone. That's how close we were. This diversion allowed our little boat to pass.

Many lost their lives on the YMS-481, but the Cofer saved 19 men. Two of the Cofer's LCVP boats went to the aid of the survivors and another YMS that had also been hit by the shore batteries.

As for our boat #2, every one aboard the Cofer had given up on us completely. The ship's log had the four of us, Walter Whitaker, Gilbert D. Crippen, William E. Flippo, and myself as missing in action. But, after a long ride two-thirds the way around Tarakan Island, we arrived back at the Cofer around 2000 hours. We were really welcomed back at the Cofer, taken to the galley, and fed well.

Something funny to us later that wasn't so funny at the time...we remembered that as our small boat was moving through the narrow strait, a short distance before coming into the large harbor, it had started lightning over the island. Every time a streak of lightning would shoot across the sky, the four of us would duck at what seemed like the gun flashes we had experienced before. We were that paranoid. This was my worst day so far of the war.

Thursday—May 3, 1945
Today was a day of transferring the YMS-481 survivors to the cruiser USS Phoenix (CL-46). The injured were transferred to the USS (LCS-50). Our LCVP boats continued minesweeping on the back side of Tarakan Island during daylight hours.

8

Saturday—May 5, 1945
We are finally leaving the Tarakan area. I am sure everyone felt as I did...we were all relieved to be leaving. There were a number of ships in the convoy leaving Tarakan. There were 20 LCIs, 8 YMSs, one Destroyer—the USS Waller (DD-466), one British ship—the HMA Burdekin (K-376), and the PC-1120. The Cofer, as usual, did the zigzagging patrol for the entire convoy. We got up to a top speed of 9.5 knots, which was a little better than usual.

Sunday—May 6, 1945
The Cofer and the Destroyer NSS Waller (DD-466) continued escorting the convoy heading towards Morotai Island, which was to be our next stop.

Monday—May 7, 1945
Still cruising toward Morotai Island at speeds from 6 knots to a maximum of 9.5 knots.

Tuesday—May 8, 1945
Our convoy spent the day cruising toward Morotai Island. We arrived at 1610 hours and anchored. By 1915 hours, all was secured. To us, today was a day to relax in a friendly port. Even so, we stood our wartime watches.

Wednesday—May 9, 1945
Another day for us to feel that we were out of the war. Even so, they had us chipping the deck and painting; first the yellow prime coat and then the Navy gray. We took on diesel fuel and furnished fresh water to two YMS ships.

Thursday—May 10, 1945
Today was another relaxing work day—fun, compared to recent days. It was also a big day for taking on ammunition after all the firing that had gone on in the Tarakan area. We received 100 five-inch 38 shells, powder, etc., plus 3,000 rounds of 30-caliber, 4200 rounds of 50-caliber and 40-millimeter shells. The 50-caliber

guns were, I believe, given to us by the Army, which we welded all around the ship onto every railing post. We used the 30-caliber and 50-caliber guns when trying to down Kamikaze planes before they could dive into our ship.

Friday—May 11, 1945
Maintained regular port anchor and usual in-port activities. We continued to stand wartime Navy watch and worked at chipping paint, buffing metal to a bright finish on the deck, and painting yellow and then normal dark gray.

Saturday—May 12, 1945
Still anchored at Morotai Island. Ships present: Allied Marines and merchantmen plus the USS Rocky Mount (AGC-3). At 0830 hours, the Captain held topside inspection of ammunition boxes and magazines, and all was cleared by 1115 hours.

Sunday—May 13, 1945
We were still anchored at Morotai Island. At 1100 hours, by order of the Comtrans Division, our top commander of our 5 APDs (the USS Kephart (APD-59), the USS Liddle (APD-60), the USS (APD-61), the USS Cofer (APD-62), and the USS Lloyd (APD-63)) held meritorious mast for the following boat crewman for successfully completing eight assault landings in the Philippines:

C. D. Crippen—Engineer
R.A. Dehart—Gunner
P.J. Douglas—Signalman
W.E. Flippo—Gunner
H. Hunter—Coxswain
A.R. Kolthoff—Engineer
C.L. League—Gunner
C.D. Mead—Engineer
A.T. Moore—Coxswain
Z. Rosenberg—Signalman
M. Santone—Engineer
J.R. Snellen—Signalman
J.E. Wajeraki—Signalman
W. Whitaker—Coxswain (note: one missing)

There were sixteen of us, plus Boat Officer E.J. McClendan. We received this commendation for always putting the initial troops ashore—one load for each of our four LCVP small landing craft. We put about 140 troops ashore in each invasion.

The four other APDs had usually been with us on each Philippine invasion except for the USS Liddle (APD-60)— knocked out of service at Ormac Bay, Leyte Island at 1202 hours on December 7, 1944.

Monday—May 14-15, 1945
Still anchored at Morotai Island.

Wednesday—May 16, 1945
At 0445 hours, a number of men who had been aboard for temporary duty were transferred off the Cofer. Other than this, no activity. Still anchored at Morotai.

Saturday—May 26, 1945
We finally received orders to get underway for firing exercises. The Cofer fired hundreds of rounds of ammunition at a towed target by an American plane. All aboard knew what lay ahead of us when we would start north to Okinawa and then next to a planned invasion of Japan. We needed to be prepared.

Monday—May 28, 1945
There was little activity today except to give fresh water to a couple of LSM ships and accept a few naval officers for temporary duty. For the next two days we remained at anchor at Morotai.

Wednesday—May 30, 1945
At 1605 hours, we accepted a number of Navy personnel aboard for temporary duty in connection with our LCVP boat's minesweeping duties. I cannot remember now, but I assume we were to teach them how we had been minesweeping in our small boats. We were now quite experienced!

Thursday—May 31, 1945
All we did today was shift anchor spots and take aboard at least another 20 temporary assignment Navy people and enlisted men. Most of them were boatswains.

Friday—June 1, 1945
The Cofer set special sea detail to get underway again and refueled at 0810 hours from the SS Bishopdale, taking aboard 14,926 gallons of fuel. At 1400 hours, Lt. Commander D.W. Blakeslee transferred to the USS Wasaton for planning

minesweeping operations. After this, the Cofer anchored again.

Saturday—June 2, 1945
Today the Cofer set off from Morotai, en route to Brunei Bay for additional minesweeping duties at 1200 hours. Our ship was part of a minesweeping convoy consisting of 6 AM steel newer-type minesweepers, 13 YMS older wooden minesweepers, 28 LCI (Landing Craft Infantry), 1 LSM (Landing Ship Medium type amphibious assault ships), and the Kline (APD-120). We could only travel at five knots because of these slower ships. The Cofer and the Kline screened the convoy by zigzagging.

Sunday—June 3, 1945
Still en route to Brunei Bay, Borneo; now up to 9 knots.

Thursday—June 7, 1945
Six days later, we arrived at Laban Island in Brunei Bay, Borneo at 1053 hours. Then we were underway again at 1530 hours.

Friday—June 8, 1945
At 0722 hours, our four boats transferred a repairs party and medical officer from the Cofer to the USS Salute (AM-294) that had hit a mine. The USS Salute quickly sank in the Brunei Bay Harbor. The Cofer later rescued 59 survivors, 42 of whom were injured.

While bombs were falling all around us, our crew members would be performing burial services to prepare the dead for burial. The bodies were placed in heavy canvas with two five-inch projectiles to make the bodies sink. The Captain would read the final prepared words for each dead sailor, ending with "I now commit this body to the deep." (My words may not be exact, but almost at least). It would be a horrible sound hearing the body wrapped in the heavy canvas sliding off the stretcher toward the water. We did this each time at Tarakan, Balikpapan, and Brunei also. All killed on the YMS minesweepers and the AM boats had to be prepared and buried by the Cofer because we were their flag ship. It seemed like we were burying guys from these YMS minesweepers almost every night.

Saturday—June 9, 1945
At 0745 hours, our four small boats were again in the water for minesweeping and returned back aboard the Cofer at 1200 hours. We then transferred a large number of Salute crew members and other minesweeping men to the USS

Phoenix (CL-46).

Sunday—June 10, 1945
At 0733 hours, all four of our LCVPs with sixteen men and one officer shoved off from the Cofer for our minesweeping duties along the proposed landing beaches.

After we returned to our ship, the USS Lloyd (APD-63) brought our mail to us. This was always a big deal to receive our mail. Often it could be several weeks before mail could catch up with us. The saddest part would be to watch someone who received very little or no mail.

Monday—June 11, 1945
Today the Cofer was anchored in Brunei Bay with various U.S. and Australian ships. She pulled anchor at 1200 hours and got underway for Tawi Tawi. We were steaming and screening the convoy with speeds up to 20 knots, all under secret dispatch. We later anchored at Rusukan Island, Brunei Bay.

Tuesday—June 12, 1945
At 1700 hours, we took aboard a number of YMS minesweeping men.

Wednesday—June 13, 1945
While anchored at Sangasiapu Island and Thumb Hill Island, a great tragedy happened today. Five of us were in LCVP boat #3 that had gone ashore to pick up a load of hemp rope. When the boat was hoisted aboard the Cofer, Don Mericle, Gunner's Mate, 3rd Class, and I got off of the boat onto the boat deck. Joe White, Seaman 1st Class, started to get out of boat #3 before it was raised another approximate ten feet to go over a steel davit then drop down into the storage cradle. Two men had to ride over the top to put in the pins that would secure the lock before the boat came down into the cradle. So Don and I pushed Joe White, who was not a member of our boat crew and really had no business being in the boat from the beginning, back into the boat. I said, "Joe, ride over like we 'Old Salts' do." (If you've been in the Navy for a while, you become an "Old Salt.") It was not a nice trip up and over the beam while the boat was being let down into the cradle.

At 1325 hours, while hoisting LCVP Boat #3 loaded with heavy rope onto the Cofer (the same boat that Joe White was in), the davit cable on the starboard side broke for the fourth time. The boat hit the top of the hoist and fell approximately twenty-five feet into the water. Meanwhile, the beam which held the pulleys and cables came out of the end sockets. This 7 ½ ton steel beam came crashing down onto boat #3, which had landed in the water with three men still in it.

My first thought when that cable broke was the fact that Mericle and I had forced poor Joe White to remain in the boat when he shouldn't have been there in the first place. But when the steel beam hit the boat, Joe luckily got thrown overboard. I jumped from the Cofer's deck, about 15 feet down into the water, and caught Joe White when he submerged. When I got to him, he was barely conscious and moaning. I caught him under his chin and grabbed the exhaust pipe of the sinking boat. Someone from the fantail threw me a donut and pulled us to the fantail. Luckily, it turned out that Joe only had a broken collar bone. I felt so badly—it was a prank that almost cost someone his life.

Another sailor aboard, Zalman Rosenberg, Signalman, 3rd Class, a red headed Jewish man in his twenties from New York City, was crushed when the beam hit boat #3. Much to our horror, when Zalman was pulled from the boat wreckage, his red hair had turned completely white. Nobody could believe this, but we all saw it with our very own eyes. Some said his hair had maybe turned white out of fright.

Also in the boat when the davit broke was my good friend, William E. Flippo, Seaman, 1st Class. Flippo was rescued and laid out on the fantail of the Cofer, and I stood and watched as they worked to resuscitate him for a few minutes. His body started turning gray and his eyes had rolled back in his head. I could not stand to watch my best friend die, so I walked away. (Remember, this Flippo was my best friend from the day we met at Fort Pierce, Florida. We were as close as two people could be.)

After boat #3 sank, boat #1 had to be transferred to the USS Pocomoke (AV-9) because the davit used to hoist the two boats onto the ship was completely gone.

At 1745 hours, we got underway to Tawi Tawi in Balikipapan, Borneo. At 1900 hours, all engines stopped during the burial service for Zalman Rosenberg, Signalman 3rd Class. He was buried at sea in 200 fathoms of water.

Friday—June 15, 1945
This was certainly a sad day for the Cofer. We went on toward our assignment at Balikipapan, Borneo. But, I could not get Flippo out of my mind. I later learned that our medical team had revived Flippo and he was alive—he didn't pass away like I had originally assumed. He was seriously injured with a broken back, broken pelvis, and leg injuries and had been transferred to the USS Pocomoke (A-19) for further medical treatment. So, when he was transferred to a hospital at our home base of Leyte, I had to see him. He was in a naval hospital on Samar Island. I caught a ride on an LCI and went to the hospital. When I walked up to his bed, he said something that I will never forget. He said, "Why did you walk away from

me when I lay wounded on the fantail?" Naturally, I explained that I wasn't able to stand around and watch him die. (But it proved something to me; even if someone is dying, they still may know what is going on!)

Flippo was the best friend that I had aboard ship. I stayed at his bedside for several hours before having to return with the LCI to the Cofer. (After discharge, he was married and named his first son after me—what an honor! I have always been sorry that I was unable to really do something big for his son when he graduated from high school, but at that time I was financially unable to do what I wished I had done. I visited Flippo two or three times in the VA Hospital in Memphis. Also, my wife, our daughter, and I visited Flippo and his wife in his later years in Mississippi.)

On the way back to the LCI, I experienced something that many people cannot imagine in their worst dreams. It was dark and I must have taken a wrong turn while walking back to the boat. All of a sudden, I found myself walking into a leper colony. I could see people with whole chunks missing from their arms or their heads. It scared the wits out of me and I flew out of there as fast as my feet would carry me. I never did tell anyone aboard about my misadventure. But I later overheard a few other sailors talking about what would happen if a person did stumble into one of these leper colonies on the island—he would be quarantined for an extended period of time. I am glad that I never mentioned my experience to anyone.

Saturday—June 16, 1945
The Cofer arrived at Point Oakland off Balikipapan, Borneo and dropped anchor. Since we had lost our two starboard boats, #1 and #3, we only had boats #2 and #4 left. Flippo had been a gunner on our boat #2. At 0315 hours, boat #2 and #4 shoved off for minesweeping duties—our first minesweeping off the Balikipapan beaches.

Flippo was replaced by a regular crew member named Douglas from Boston, Massachusetts. As we lost people, they'd take regular crewmen and put them in the boat crew. I don't remember how old he was, but many of our replacements were older—around 35 or 40. They were old to us!

At 1330 hours, a board led by Lt. Charles H. Cofer came to inquire into the davit tragedy.

Sunday—June 17, 1945
The Cofer moved around the Balikipapan harbor and shifted anchor several times today. Japanese planes appeared on radar more than once, sending us to General Quarters.

Monday—June 18, 1945
Today the Cofer played mother ship to a number of YMS minesweepers assigned to this Balikipapan operation. At 1300 hours, the YMS-50 hit a mine and was dead in the water. Our two remaining LCVP boats were sent out to pick up the 23 survivors and transferred them to the USS Montpelier (CL-57). Meanwhile, Jap planes suddenly appeared from different directions. One was an enemy float plane that the Cofer shot down at 1855 hours.

Tuesday—June 19, 1945
This was a typical day going to General Quarters before sunrise, dropping anchor, and then chipping rust and painting the ship. We anchored in the northwest corner of the area known as the Cardinals. As usual, we went to General Quarters several times when Japanese bogies showed up on radar.

Wednesday—June 20, 1945
A mine exploded near the YMS-368, sustaining a damaged hull and three casualties. Unidentified aircraft seemed to be appearing regularly.

Thursday—June 21, 1945
Today the YMS minesweepers came under fire from shore batteries. The YMS-335 was hit and sustained casualties, which were picked up by our two LCVP boats to transfer to the USS Montpelier (CL-57).

Friday—June 22, 1945
At 0810 hours, the YMS-53 was tied up to the Cofer's port side and the YMS-369 to our starboard side. Again, we were the mother ship to these minesweepers. At 1014 hours, the YMS-10 was hit on her bow by enemy fire from the beach. Luckily there were no casualties, only a hole in the bow.

Later at 1658 hours, the YMS-58 was fired on from the beach. Lt. J.G. Charles Cohen later came aboard for temporary duty pertaining to our small boat minesweeping duties. I don't know why this was necessary because we had our boat officer McClendon already, and we had done minesweeping duties elsewhere in Brunei Bay and Tarakan, Borneo.

Saturday—June 23, 1945
All survivors from the YMS-50 were transferred to the USS Chepachet (A-078) today. The Balikipapan harbor, now named Kelimantan Providence, Indonesia, was one of the biggest oil fields in Asia—taken over in 1942 by the Japanese. The oil was of such good quality that you could put it right on a ship without refinery.

The Japanese had taken over similar oil supply areas in Brunei Bay and Tarakan also. When they Japanese saw our convoy approaching, they set fire to the huge tanks of oil to prevent Allies from getting at their oil.

Sunday—June 24, 1945
Today started out as our usual busy minesweeping duties. But at 2027 hours, all hell broke loose as Jap torpedo planes came at the Cofer. Our leaders thought they were "Bettys"—a type of Japanese torpedo bomber. One plane passed directly over our mid-ship from starboard to port at an estimated 50 feet above the Cofer. I was the caller for the 20-mm gun on the starboard side next to the bridge. When the Gunnery Officer gave the command to start firing, I was to pass on the information to the gunner who was strapped to the gun. He would not fire until he was given the "okay" from the bridge. When I received the message to commence firing, I reached over to hit him on the back to relay the message and realized that he had deserted his battle station. I jumped over and took his position, but I was too late; the plane had already flown over us and dropped a torpedo. Thankfully, it went completely under the Cofer and out the port side while two others passed ahead of the Cofer. The plane was hit on its right engine by the Cofer and crashed into the sea.

As for the gunner who had deserted his gun—there's no telling what they would have done to him if I would have reported it. But I didn't, and I won't mention his name even now. Our ship made hard turns one way and the other and eight torpedoes reportedly missed our ship that day, while two planes were shot down.

Another one of our shipmates, who will also remain nameless by me, jumped overboard when the plane dropped that torpedo. He treaded water for approximately one and a half hours before the YMS-364 reported hearing someone calling out. Fifteen minutes later, LCVP boat #4 was lowered into the water and found him. He could have also been court martialed, but wasn't.

Monday—June 25, 1945
Still at Balikipapan, Borneo. During the day, our two LCVP boats would mine sweep along the Balikipapan beaches. At night, we would escort the demolition boys, known as "Demo Boys" (now called the Seals) to the beaches. We would put our boats on underwater exhaust to come in as quietly as possible and then the Demo Boys would jump overboard and swim to the targeted beach. They had on nothing but their swim trunks and what I will call "web feet" for swimming with all kinds of ammunition strapped to their waist. They had certain targets they were directed to hit. And hit them, they did! As I remember, radio stations were

their main target. After about 30 minutes, we would hear explosions and we knew they had hit their targets. Shortly afterwards, we would see a small blinking light on the beach, and we rushed to pick them up. This went on for days before the Australians and Dutch troops would make their landing at Balikipapan. To the best of my knowledge, our demolition teams did not lose a single man at Borneo. What they did was unreal.

Tuesday—June 26, 1945

I can not remember how and when we left Balikipapan, Borneo, but today, we were back en route to Balikipapan accompanied by the following YMS ships: #10, 46, 47, 49, 50, 53, 95, 315, 335, 336, 364, 368, and 392, plus the USS Gualala (AGG). The Cofer was the flag ship for these minesweepers because we had a high ranking officer aboard who was responsible for this operation.

At 0708 hours, we anchored again back at Point Oakland off Balikipapan, Borneo. The YMS-50 was hit again by a mine and was pronounced dead in the water. Boats #2 and #4 were lowered into the water and went to rescue the injured. At 1542 hours, our boats returned with 23 survivors from the YMS-50 and at 1400 hours, boats #2 and #4 returned from minesweeping duty.

Lt. Charles H. Cofer, along with senior members, convened for an inquiry into the davit boat tragedy. This was the accident that killed Zalman Rosenberg, injuring William E. Flippo and Joe R. White.

Earlier today, an unidentified plane closed in at 17 miles, then suddenly disappeared from radar. Later, another plane appeared on radar and this one identified as friendly. Every time, day or night, when bogies appeared on radar, we would be sent to General Quarters until identified. Again, at 2000 hours, enemy planes were detected by radar, dropping bombs on our group, but no damage was done. By 2055 hours, all was secured from General Quarters.

Wednesday—June 27, 1945

Today we furnished fresh water to several YMS ships—the YMS-49, YMS-53, and YMS-368. Our ship had the ability to de-salt sea water and the Cofer furnished the YMS ships with fresh water as needed. Even though our ship had the de-salting capabilities, we Cofer people still had to shower in salt water, which is extremely rough on the skin! The Navy even had brown salt water soap. I always wondered why the Cofer gave away fresh water when we had to shower in salt water. No wonder they called us "Old Salts."

At 1014 hours, the YMS-10 was hit by shore fires, but no casualties were reported. Bigger minesweepers like the AM-299, USS Scout (AM-296), USS LSML, YMS-314, YMS-39, and YMS-365 joined our group.

The YMS-335 was hit by shore batteries at 1455 hours and boat #4 showed up to assist with casualties; taking them to the USS Montplier (CL-57).

The YMS-365 was struck by a mine. It sustained severe damage with six casualties. YMS-364 placed their injured aboard the USS Columbia (CL-56).

At 1547 hours, YMS-39 hit a mine and sank. My boat #2 left the ship with a rescue party to pick up survivors, which we transferred to the USS Schmidt (APD 76).

Thursday—June 28, 1945
At 0740 hours, our boat #2 was lowered into the water, 15 miles east of Balikipapan, Borneo to act as a standby rescue boat. At 1415 hours, the YMS-47 was struck by a mine and sustained severe hull damage with two injured. Boat #4 picked up the three casualties and brought them to the Cofer. The YMS-49 took the YMS-47 in tow to an anchorage area.

Friday—June 29, 1945
Our two LCVP boats were again kept very busy today. First an American B-25 crashed near the beach at 1250 hours. Our boat, #2, and boat #4 and the USS Stevens (DD-479) picked up one survivor each, who were then taken to the USS Montpelier. We transferred the casualties from the USS-47 to the USS Columbia (CL-55). Then at 0715 hours, our boat #2 put in the water and again proceeded to an area known as the Phillies. The Cofer anchored while waiting for my boat #2 to return. Finally, it was decided that my boat would spend the night tied to the USS Sentry (AM-299).

Sunday—July 1, 1945
Today was the big day in Balikipapan as it was invasion day—"D-Day"! Borneo had previously been a Dutch providence, so the Australians and Dutch troops were the invading troops while the Americans did the minesweeping patrolling. The Cofer had been here since June 15th, so much of our minesweeping duties were finished. Today was mostly patrolling and observing what went on with the invasion.

Once the Australian Infantry took over Borneo, the Japanese would be left with no oil.

Tuesday—July 3, 1945
At 0430 hours, anchored off Balikipapan, we were called to battle stations as four approaching enemy planes appeared on radar. One was shot down 40 miles out from the Cofer.

Thursday—July 5, 1945
We were still anchored and at 0628 hours, all ships were ordered to lay a smoke screen as bogies approached.

Sunday—July 8, 1945
At 0700 hours, my boat, #2, and boat #4 were put in the water for minesweeping. At 1350 hours, the YMS-84 struck a mine. The YMS-367 later towed the YMS-84 out of the water but at 1540 hours, it sank.

Tuesday—July 10, 1945
All 34 survivors from the YMS-84 were taken aboard the Cofer today. After 25 days in this area, we left Balikipapan for our home port of Leyte. Our experiences in Balikipapan were something to remember.

Friday—July 14, 1945
The Cofer arrived back in the Leyte area and transferred the YMS-84 survivors to the US Navy receiving station in Leyte.

Saturday—July 15, 1945
Still anchored back in our home port of Leyte Gulf. It was a day of relaxing and beach parties. Because we had to maintain a stand-by crew in case of an emergency, they would only allow a certain number of us to go ashore at one time. The Navy rules said no drinking aboard ship. However after dark, they would often pass out beer once the Cofer was underway, but never in port, as I remember.

Sunday—July 16, 1945
Another uneventful day while anchored in the Leyte harbor. The USS Idaho (BB-42) battleship was present. This was a beautiful site for us to see. Compared to our 306-foot Cofer and other ships in our 7th Fleet, the 624-foot Idaho was larger than what we were accustomed to seeing.

July 17-25, 1945
Still anchored in Leyte Gulf, which is a real treat to us—sort of a vacation after what we had been accustomed to in Balikipapan.

Thursday—July 26, 1945
Today Walter Maki, Radioman, 2nd Class, and Manuel Mendendez, Radioman, 3rd Class, who later became personal friends during our many reunions, were transferred from the Cofer to be reassigned.

Saturday—July 28, 1945
Being a boat crew member, one thing that I personally looked forward to was going in our #2 boat to Tacloban City, Leyte Island to get our mail. It was often so muddy in the streets of Leyte, but the Red Cross was usually there giving out donuts and coffee. It was fun for me.

Monday—July 30, 1945
The usual chipping and painting kept us busy, especially when in port.

Thursday—August 2, 1945
Today we took on 69,685 gallons of fuel.

Friday—August 3, 1945
We transferred 1,500 gallons of our diesel fuel to the USS LCS.

Monday—August 6, 1945
As we lay anchored in the Leyte harbor, the United States dropped the atomic bomb at 0815 hours on Hiroshima, Japan.

Thursday—August 9, 1945
Three days later, another atomic bomb was dropped on Nagasaki, Japan at 1102 hours.

Friday—August 10, 1945
One thing was different for us today—the Captain held a ship's inspection. This was never done in battle areas.

Sunday—August 12, 1945
Today we entered the floating dry dock, USS (ARD-16). I am not sure why the dry dock was necessary.

Monday—August 13, 1945
I learned today why we were in the floating dry dock. It was to repair the injection line, the hull, and get a basic overhaul.

Tuesday—August 14, 1945
The Cofer's boilers were lit off in preparation to leave the dry dock. At 0816 hours we were out and clear of the dry dock.

Wednesday—August 15, 1945
Back to anchor in the Leyte harbor and back to our usual chipping paint and repainting.

Friday—August 17, 1945
Today was another ship's inspection day and testing of all ammunition box areas and sprinkler system. The Cofer's sprinkler system was so important in case of a hit.

Saturday—August 18, 1945
There are big rumors that we are getting ready to participate in the invasion of Japan. Okinawa was pretty secure by now. Our convoy missed the Okinawa invasion because we were in Borneo. I don't know which would have been worse—the suicide planes hitting the Navy at Okinawa or working with our Navy's minesweepers in Borneo. The minesweeping duties along the enemy beaches were definitely no picnic.

Sunday—August 19, 1945
Today the rumors are confirmed—next we were to load troops for Okinawa, and then it is off to Japan.

Monday—August 20, 1945
After spending more than a month in Leyte, we pulled anchor and headed for Guiyan Roadstead, Samar.

Tuesday—August 21, 1945
Anchored among many Allied ships. Also present was the Battleship USS Idaho (BB-42).

Wednesday—August 22, 1945
At 1035 hours, we pulled anchor and headed back to the Leyte Harbor, arriving

back at 1420 hours.

Thursday—August 23, 1945
Other than magazine inspections, all normal today.

Tuesday—August 28, 1945
The USS Carter (LSD-3) landing ship dock picked up two new LCVPs and placed them in the cradles aboard our ship on the starboard side. Remember, the boom broke earlier, wounding two and killing Signalman Rosenberg. The Cofer was left with no boom to lift the boats, so the USS Carter lifted the two boats aboard to keep the balance of our ship. We looked funny with two boats on our port side and empty spots on the starboard side.

9

Wednesday—August 29, 1945
Today was as we suspected—our big day! We were finally headed for Buckner Bay, Okinawa, accompanied by the following ships from Division #103: USS Lloyd (APD-63), USS Newman (APD-59), USS Kephart (APD-61), the Dianchenko (APD-12), and our guide ship, the USS Liddle (APD-60), back from repairs in San Francisco. We conducted all sorts of war time exercises while en route.

Thursday—August 30, 1945
Our convoy was still underway, heading toward Buckner Bay, Okinawa, cruising at 16 knots, maintaining war-cruising watches and tests.

Saturday—September 1, 1945
At 0842 hours, we passed through the gate entrance at Buckner Bay, Okinawa, anchoring at 0919 hours. The Cofer took on fuel from the tanker USS Clostic (IX-137) later today. Okinawa had already been taken over and was secure, but there continued to be a constant threat of suicide planes.

Sunday—September 2, 1945
Remained anchored in Buckner Bay, Okinawa. Buckner Bay was named after General Buckner who was killed in the battle for Okinawa. I was told that he was the highest ranking general killed. (I believe this included only the South Pacific, but I am not sure.)

Monday—September 3, 1945
Today marked the end of World War II. Surprisingly, however, our official ship's log made no such mention. I guess for the Captain, even though we were not technically at war, things had not changed.

Tuesday—September 4, 1945
We were still standing war-time watches as if the war was still going strong. At 1600 hours, the Cofer was ordered to report to the 5th Fleet Commander who was

aboard the USS New Jersey (BB-62). As enlisted men, we knew nothing of what would be happening during the next few days, but we suspected something big was in the works.

Wednesday—September 5, 1945
Lieutenant Charles Cofer was transferred off the Cofer to state side for separation. Lt. Walter Meredith took over as Executive Officer to replace Lieutenant Cofer.

Thursday—September 6, 1945
Nothing happened today. As the Cofer sat in Buckner Bay, we were all on edge to see what would happen to us next. Peace was signed in Tokyo and we knew, without a doubt, that we would be going somewhere else soon. As enlisted men, we were always the last to know anything.

Friday—September 7, 1945
Still wondering what next!

Saturday—September 8, 1945
Today we refueled. For the first time, to my knowledge, we took on fresh water from the USS Sobarisseu (AO-93). This was strange because we were usually the one to furnish fresh water to smaller ships. Now, fully loaded with fuel and fresh water, we were ready for something. No doubt, our Captain and Executive Officer knew what was next.

Sunday—September 9, 1945
We were finally informed of our destination. At 1230 hours, we were underway and secured for special sea detail, still at war-cruising speed. Our ship was accompanied by USS Lunga Point (CVE-94); USS Montpelier (CL-57), whom we were familiar with from Borneo; USS Cabildo (LSD-16); USS Consolation (AH-15); USS Sanctuary (AH-17); screened by USS McGinty (DE-365); USS Cockrell (DE-366); USS C.S. Doyle (DE-368); USS Frencid (DE-367); and the USS Tatum (APD-81), all in formation with several hospital ships en route to Wakayama, Honshu Island, Japan to evacuate Allied prisoners of war.

Monday—September 10, 1945
Today our convoy continued en route to Wakayama.

Tuesday–September 11, 1945

At 0615 hours, the Cofer decreased speeds to five knots while tying up to the rendezvous area. A Japanese pilot came aboard our American ship to steer us through the mine fields. All was tense with a Japanese sailor piloting our ship. We were forced to inspect ammunition magazines, smoke screen powder samples, and to be alert for anything.

Wednesday–September 12, 1945

Today was another cautious day, staying on alert and testing all ammunition magazines and smokeless powder. Because we were not sure what to expect from Japan, the Captain had all free hands top side with life jackets on. We were always required to wear our life jackets while at battle stations. Otherwise, the safest place aboard the ship in a mine field was top side.

Thursday–September 13, 1945

Again all were alert.

Saturday–September 15, 1945

The Cofer led six hospital ships up through the channel to Wakayama, Japan. The first afternoon in Wakayama was something for us! A few weeks ago, the Japanese were our enemies and now, here we are, anchored in their harbor. Wakayama had not been hit by the atomic bombs and the city was in excellent condition.

The commanding group of our ships asked for volunteers to go ashore in order to set up a radio station to accept the former Allied prisoners of war that were due tomorrow. I volunteered, as did sixteen others. It was a tense period as we walked toward the hotel where the radio station was to be set up. We were the first Americans who had walked ashore at Wakayama and they were frightened people.

Apparently, many Japanese had been assigned to clean up the hotel in preparation for the arrival of the POWs who had previously been held by the Japanese. It was odd seeing the Japanese sitting cross-legged along the sidewalk as we walked up to the hotel with something like a machete beside them.

Our group of volunteers spent the night at the Japanese hotel and early the next morning, we heard a train coming around the mountain with its whistles wide open. Looking out upon this train was a site I will never forget. There were former POWs hanging out of just about every window, waving little American flags. This was their first time seeing American ships in years. (I always wondered where the men had gotten these American flags, but I guess they had been parachuted onto the POW camps.)

All of the POWs coming aboard our ship appeared to be in good shape and the hospital ships received those needing medical attention. I later talked to many of these POWs while en route back to Okinawa. Most did appear to be in reasonably good health, except almost all had "Beri-Beri"—something that I had never heard of before. They would push on their legs and it would seem forever before the skin would come back to where it was before. They said it was due to malnutrition. They told me the only food they had been served was rice. One of the POWs named Maggard from my home state of Kentucky gave me a white wool blanket stamped with the US Navy seal that had been dropped by American planes on their Japanese POW camp. I treasure and still have that blanket.

Many said they had worked in coal mines and the managers had often called them to their homes one at a time. Most said they had not been treated too badly, even though we had heard rumor of other POW locations where the prisoners were badly mistreated.

The Cofer then returned to Okinawa with approximately 135 Allied ex-prisoners of war.

Sunday—September 16, 1945

Today the Cofer left Okinawa for Nagasaki, Japan for evacuations of more Allied ex-POWs. Nagasaki was the second Japanese city hit with an atomic bomb called "Fat Man."

Monday—September 17, 1945

The Cofer arrived in Nagasaki today. The United States dropped the atomic bomb at 11:02 a.m. on August 9, 1945—only 5 weeks ago. The heat from the blast instantly killed about 70,000 of Nagasaki's 240,000 residents. Even the people who managed to survive continue to suffer from the effects from the radiation poisoning such as leukemia and caner even today. It destroyed most of the houses and buildings within a 1.5 mile radius.

Nagasaki was a city in the harbor and the bomb had been dropped right in the center of the town. We spent five days in Nagasaki tied up to what had once been concrete ship docks in the heart of the city. It was a sad place—there was no town left, but we were allowed to walk freely through the ruins of the city. The places that had once been streets were now bulldozed into big open areas. The smell was awful.

More than anything, I wanted a souvenir from Nagasaki, and I found one. A bank vault had been blown to pieces and lying out in the open was a book marked the "Bank of Nagasaki Code Book, 1938." I still have that book here at my home. At the time, it was undoubtedly hot, but at the time, we knew nothing about radiation. I kept that book in my locker aboard ship for the remainder of my service.

Tuesday—September 18, 1945
The Cofer was still tied up in Nagasaki. All crew members were horrified at the sight of what had once been a city, demolished by the atomic bomb that the U.S. had dropped on Nagasaki.

Wednesday—September 19, 1945
We were moored alongside the USS Gilmer (APD-11) at Nagasaki's harbor. Our LSVP boats, #2, and #4 were used to patrol around the Cofer. Some of the recovered former Allied POW military personnel came aboard our ship.

Thursday—September 20, 1945
Still in the Nagasaki harbor. Our Captain always remained alert by having us go through ammunition inspections and testing smoke samples. The war was over, but we continued to be cautious.

Friday—September 21, 1945
140 additional British and American former POWs came aboard the Cofer.

Saturday—September 22, 1945
Early this morning we were making preparations to get underway for Okinawa with our load of former POWs. I'm attaching a two page list of those whom we took aboard. More than 100 are from Great Britain.

At 1005 hours, we were underway and all were anxious to leave Nagasaki. This was a place we would never forget. Even though peace was signed, while en route to Okinawa, we were still operating under war conditions.

The following two pages are a list of British POWs that we rescued from Nagasaki, Japan on September 22, 1945.

DECK LOG—REMARKS SHEET

UNITED STATES SHIP ___ CUR__ (APD 62) ___ Friday 21 September 1945

0000-0400:
Moored alongside USS GILMER (APD 11) in berth 1 south in harbor of Nagasaki, Kyushu, Japan. Ships present: various units of allied navies comprising Nagasaki evacuation and occupation group. CTG 55.7 in USS WICHITA (CA 45) SOPA. #1 boiler in operation for auxiliary purposes. Maintaining in port and deck security watches. Average steam 430#.

_____ Cleland,
Lieut. D, USNR.

0400-0800:
Moored as before. Average steam 470#.

H. C. Stubbs,
Lieut. (jg) USN.

0800-1200:
Moored as before. 0815 Mustered crew on stations; no absentees. 0900 Made daily inspection of magazines, ready boxes and smokeless powder samples; conditions normal. Made weekly tests of magazine sprinkling systems; test satisfactory. 1005 Made all regular preparations to get underway. 1020 Set special sea detail. 1033 Underway on various courses and speeds to no alongside Dejima Pier, Nagasaki, Kyushu, Japan. 1066 Moored starboard side to Dejima Pier. 1106 Secured from special sea detail, set in port watch. 1110 In accordance with CTG 55.7, 2215 I, TBS measure following officers and men were transferred to USS TOMILE (CL 63): Lt. Col. R. _. SCHOTT, O-329774, USA; Lieut. Edward M. LITTLE, 63373, USN; TRYLER, J., M/Sgt. USA and O'FERRO Oscar, Pv. USA. Average steam 430#.

E. M. Dumont
Rev. O(L), USNR.

1200-1600:
Moored as before. 1220 Secured #2 boiler and #1 and #2 main engines. 1535 The following Recovered Allied Military Personnel came aboard for transporation:

ARMSTRONG, Harold, 13056422, L/Cpl. Brit. Army;
BARBER, Herbert K. 16015573, Sgt. U.S. Army;
BEATON, Francis J. 16397274, Bdr. Brit. Army
BEDLEY, Hancock, 1737844, L/Bdr. Brit. Army
BIRNES, Geo. W., 287 42 27, GM2c. U.S. Navy
BLOOMFIELD, Alfred, 1573334, Gun. Brit. Army
BOOTH, A.H., 1807728, Gun. Brit. Army
BOYER, Franklin, 2186%, Cpl., U.S.M.C.
BRAY, Edwin J., 1611704, Gun. Brit. Army
BREWS, Robert 1568446, Gun. Brit. Army
CAMPBELL, Iain 5122875, Pvt. Brit. Army
CARLESS, Tom 10631274, Gun. Brit. Army
CARLTON, Hanford P. 261673, Pfc. U.S.M.C.
CLARKE, John R. 13056440, Gun. Brit. Army
CLARKE, Wm., 1822032, Gun. Brit. Army
CONNOR, John 1563203, Gun. Brit. Army
CORRIDAN, James D. O-298909, Major, U.S. Army
DUNBAR, A., 1640939, Gun. Brit. Army
DUDDITT, Frederick A. 2361377, S'. Brit. Army
DUSTEED, Chas. L., 237668, Pi/Sgt., U.S.M.C.
FARMER, Randolph P. 214410, S/Sgt. U.S. Army
FLYNN, John 1547315, Gun. Brit. Army
FRANKLIN, Chas. L., 1780365, Gun. Brit. Army
FRYETT, Frank 1471520, Rad. Brit. Army
GARNER, P. James, 1548099, Gun. Brit. Army
GRANDON, Daniel 857241, Sgt. Brit. Army
GREENBURG, A. 291115, Pvt. U.S.M.C.
HADLEY, Samuel T. 207 64 61, AS2c U.S. Navy
EATON, Leslie 1804739, Gun. Brit. Army
HARRISON, Jos. R., 1636477, Gun. Brit. Army
HAXTON, Henry G. 1625518 L/Bdr. Brit. Army
HEATH, P.R., 1154072, Cpl. Brit. Army
HOSE, Edward R. 301436, Pvt. U.S.M.C.
JONES, Henry F. 2338958 SM Brit. Army
KELLEY, C.J., 6933222, Pfc. U.S. Army
KELSEY, J.W., 234889, 3M Brit. Army
KUZALL, Wm. J. 296504, Sgt. U.S.M.C.

ASHTON, Ronald, 1738422, L/Bdr. Brit. Army;
BAKER, John, 10540249, Pvt. Brit. Army
BEET, Reginald, 233 8266, St, Brit. Army
BENNETT, Keith, 280556, Cpl., U.S.M.C.
BLANCHFIELD, Alfred, 2538102, SM, Brit. Army
BLOXER, B.W., 5770997, Driver, Brit. Army
BOYTON, Wm., 1735408, Gun. Brit. Army
BRADLEY, John, 13022744, Pvt. Brit. Army
BUCHNEL, Thomas, 276039, Driver, Brit. Army
CALVIN, Taylor P., 278993, Cpl. U.S.M.C.
CARCAS, Horace O. 1771690, Gun. Brit. Army
CARLTON, Albert S. 6344250, Gun. Brit. Army
CHICK, Fred 1717736, Gun. Brit. Army
CLARKE, Lloyd 948450, L/Bdr. Brit. Army
COLOUBER, Wm., 1818825, Gun. Brit. Army
CORNELL, Norman R. 1285412, L.A.C., Brit. Army
DESMOND, Henry 1607407, Gun. Brit. Army
DURKIN, Lloyd T. 288559, Pfc. U.S.M.C.
EASTMAN, Reuben 1618458, Bdr. Brit. Army
EDMONDS, Homer L. 23043322, Sgt. U.S. Army
FLEMING, William 1636188, L/Bdr. Brit. Army
FRACALE, Jos. F., 6904787, S/Sgt. U.S. Army
FRENDOIS, Ray M. 18015282, Pvt. U.S. Army
GARNER, Leslie K. 1491797, Gun. Brit. Army
GOODRIDGE, Ernest 1653727, Gun. Brit. Army
GREEN, Cecil 2797AA Pfc. U.S.M.C.
GRIBBEN, Wm. P. 13056164, Pvt. Brit. Army
HALLIWELL, Thomas 1685560, Gun. Brit. Army
HANSON, LeRoy 174623, T/Sgt. U.S.M.C.
HAWKINS, Edwin 1583332, Gun. Brit. Army
HAYNES, Eric S. 1807155, Gun. Brit. Army
HOPKINS, John 1821407, Gun. Brit. Army
HUGHES, Henry O. 7258669, Sgt. Brit. Army
JOSEPH, Thos. H., Gun. Brit. Army
KELLY, Michael B. 948609, S/LAC, Brit. Army
KILLIAN, Albert 1519609, Gun. Brit. Army
KNOX, Ed. M. 223 39 17, HA3c U.S. Navy

APPROVED: ___ H. C. ___, ___ R. COMMANDING
EXAMINED: ___ Meredith, Lieut., ___ R. NAVIGATOR

CONFIDENTIAL

NAVPERS 134 (REV. 1-44) PAGE 2970

DECK LOG—ADDITIONAL REMARKS SHEET

UNITED STATES SHIP COFER (APD 62) Friday 21 September 19 45
(Day) (Date) (Month)

ADDITIONAL REMARKS

1200-1600:

LEONARD, Wm. 1825997, Gun Brit. Army	LEWIS, Walter R. 2059097, L/Bdr. Brit. Army
LITTLE, Chas. 900930, L/Bdr. Brit. Army	LOCKHART, Thomas E. 272 09 43, PhM3c U.S. Navy
LONGBOTTOM, Willie, 1808232, Gun. Brit. A.	LOWE, James H. 2338548, SM, Brit. Army
LYNCH, D.J., 1491918, Sgt. Brit. Army	LAMBERT, Jack 1518084, Gun. Brit. Army
MAHONEY, Jos. R. 35001926, Pvt. U.S. Army	MC CARTHY, Patrick, 7375047, Pvt. Brit. Army
MC FARLANE, Wm. 1579943, Gun. Brit. Army	MC GOLDRICK, Francis P. 1105224, Gun. Brit. Army
MC GOVERN, John 1822391, Gun. Brit. Army	MERTES, Henry D. 6590170, Cp.3c., U.S. Army
MESSENGER, Thomas, 3819609, T.O.1c. Brit.	MILLS, Arthur R. 5116941, Cpl. Brit. Army
MOFFAT, Albert 13056385, Pvt. Brit. Army	MOORES, Frank 1619590, Gun. Brit. Army
MORRISON, Frank 1807747, Gun. Brit. Army	MULFORD, Geoffrey 1177847, A.C.1, Brit. Army
NICHOLLS, Douglas, 1441928, Bdr. Brit. A.	NICHOLSON, Warren T. 2598737, SM Brit. Army
NIXON, James D. 269092, Pvt. U.S.M.C.	OWEN, Alfred J. 1599635, Bdr. Brit. Army
OWEN, Donald 899090 Gun. Brit. Army	PAGE, Richie J. 19046009 Pfc. U.S. Army
PARTRIDGE, Wm. H. 1736559, Gun. Brit. Army	PATRICK, Fred D. 6288999 Cpl. U.S. Army
PEEK, Jack V. 6972770, U.S. Army	PERKINS, Sydney 899516 Gun. Brit. Army
POLLARD, H.S., 1519116, L/Bdr. Brit. Army	PORTER, Chester A. 207380, Cpl. U.S.M.C.
POWELL, Felix D. 266 34 34 TM2c U.S. Navy	PRUITT, Roscoe O-256298 Major, U.S. Army
PURLING, Donald T. 342 20 15 Y3c. U.S.N.	PYLE, Alfred 3193426 Gun. Brit. Army
REGINALD, Chadwick 1372953 ... Brit. Army	RICE, Norman E. 2867824, Craftsman, Brit. Army
RICHARDS, Leslie 11051591, Gun. Brit. Army	RIDINGS, Gene T. 18016736 Pvt. U.S. Army
ROBERTS, Albert W. 265 88 39 EM2c U.S.N.	ROBERTS, Stanley G. 1577161 Gun. Brit. Army
ROCHE, H.J.T. 7649027 Driver Brit. Army	SAVAGE, Cole 1706932, Driver, Brit. Army
SANDERS, James R. 6399432, Driver Brit. A.	SEWARD, H.P. 1042452, Gun. Brit. Army
SHELDON, Frank 1592427, Gun. Brit. Army	SIMS, Frederick E. 2333191, SM Brit. Army
SKINNER, Walter 13056893 Pvt. Brit. Army	SMITH, Edw. D. PL/Sgt. U.S.M.C.
SMITH Wm. 6268460 Sgt. U.S. Army	SMITH, James 1809103 Gun. Brit. Army
SNOW, Rex J. 328 72 07 EM2c US. Navy	SNYDER, Wm A. 15027526 T/Sgt. U.S. Army
SOMERS, Albert 4661288 Gun. Brit. Army	STANTON, Lionel 1643365 Gun. Brit. Army
TANNER, J.H. 279879, U.S.M.C.	VARLEY, E.C. 1735263 Gun. Brit. Army
VERNON, Sidney O-319993 Major U.S. Army	VERSAW, Donald L. 266117 Pfc. U.S.M.C.
VESEY, Eric 1821778 Gun. Brit. Army	WALLACE, Wm. 922703 Gun. Brit. Army
WATSON, Frank 1223349 L/Cpl. Brit. Army	WATSON, Glenn M. 6914475 M/Sgt. U.S. Army
WEATHERMAN, Lester L. 19003070 Pfc. U.S.A.	WELCH, Chas. R. 20229142 Pfc. U.S. Army
WELHAM, C.V. 1823373 Gun. Brit. Army	WELLINGS, Thomas 1782865 Gun. Brit. Army
WESTWOOD, Alfred V. 1580734 Gun. Brit. A.	WHITE, Wm. O. 19061982 U.S. Army
WILLIAMS, Chester 19002106 Pfc. US.Army	WILLIAMS, Frank D. 1808718, Gun. Brit. Army
WILLIAMS, Leo H. 393 03 86 Flc U.S. Navy	WILSON, Andrew A. 906985 Gun. Brit. Army
WILSON, Woodrow 6834476 Sgt. U.S.Army	WINDUST, Robert C. 790169 Sgt. Brit. Army
WITHERINGTON, Denham 1782833 Gun. Brit.	WOOD, Frederick J. 814421 Sgt. Brit. Army
WOOLLEY, Anthony A. 2060438 Gun. Brit. A.	WRIGHT, Arthur 1425231 Sgt. U.S. Army
YOUNG, William M 6852536 S/Sgt. US. Army	BENNETT, Lester C. 269220 Cpl. U.S.M.C.
SANDERS, R.H. 1409206 L/Bdr. Brit. Army	STREAMES, James 1643365 Gun. Brit. Army

Average steam 430#.

R. H. Antin
R. H. Antin,
Lieut. D, USNR.

1600-2000:
Moored as before. Average steam 430#.

P. F. Albert
P. F. Albert,
Ens. D, USNR.

2000-2400:
Moored as before. Average steam 430#.

B. Kaser
B. Kaser,
Lieut. (jg) D, USNR.

APPROVED: H. C. McGinnis, Lt. Comdr. D, U.S.N.R. COMMANDING

EXAMINED: W. C. Meredith, Lieut. D, U.S.N.R. NAVIGATOR

TO BE FORWARDED DIRECT TO THE BUREAU OF NAVAL PERSONNEL AT THE END OF EACH MONTH

Sunday—September 23, 1945
Spent the day traveling toward Okinawa, arriving about noon, and dropped anchor at 1235 hours in Buckner Bay, Okinawa.

Monday—September 24, 1945
At 1515 hours, all former POWs were transferred from the Cofer to the USS LCT-1339. Those former POWs were a happy bunch!

Tuesday—September 25, 1945
Spent the day at anchor in Buckner Bay, Okinawa.

Wednesday—September 26, 1945
A number of the Cofer crew were transferred to a receiving station ashore at Okinawa. With the war over, some of the old timers headed home for discharge.

Thursday—September 27, 1945
Today was my nineteenth birthday. I spent my entire eighteenth year at sea in the South Pacific.

At 0510 hours, the Cofer lit her boilers to get underway again. As enlisted men, once again, we had no idea where we were heading to next. As of midnight, we were still underway, heading north to Sasebo, Japan.

Tuesday—October 2, 1945
Early this morning, we moved to another location in the Sasebo Harbor. 23 of the Cofer crew transferred and headed home for discharge. Later in the day, we received orders to head back to Okinawa to pick up even more former Allied POWs.

Wednesday—October 3, 1945
For a change, the Cofer was traveling alone toward Okinawa. At 2030 hours, we dropped anchor in Hagushi, Okinawa awaiting our further orders for our next assignment.

Thursday—October 4, 1945
Still at anchor in Okinawa.

Saturday—October 6, 1945
Other than transferring one gunner's mate for passage home, there was little activity today except for our usual detail.

South Pacific at Seventeen

Monday—October 8, 1945

We again left Okinawa and as of yet, we enlisted men wondered where we are headed this time, and always wondering when we would be heading home now that the war was over.

Tuesday—October 9, 1945

We soon found out why we had pulled anchor and headed out to sea. We were given the order that all smaller ships around Okinawa had to get under way due to a typhoon that was headed for Okinawa. Some captains of the smaller ships opted to remain next to land, but orders were orders, and we were ordered to head out to sea in hope of avoiding the worst part of the storm.

Thursday—October 11, 1945

This turned out to be one horrible typhoon. It is odd that our ship's log says next to nothing about the seriousness of this typhoon. It was horrible! The Cofer was assigned to go all the way around the island and make every ship get underway as soon as possible. Some people begged us to not make them go—they didn't want to go out and face the typhoon in open waters. When we pulled out to sea, there were more than 100 ships in a convoy trying to out-run the typhoon. A number of these ships were merchant marine liberty ships and they could not travel very fast. But by daylight, there was not a single ship in sight, due to the storm and rough seas. They had gone in all directions.

Friday—October 12, 1945

By noon, our ship headed into the storm and the rough, rough seas. The winds were blowing around 90 miles per hour with 30-35 foot waves battering the ship. The Captain slowed to almost nothing in order to keep the ship headed into the waves. Luckily we never got cross ways of the waves because if we had, our top-heavy ship would have surely capsized. Our ship sustained much damage, and yet our ship's log mentions nothing—this is so strange to me.

The force of the wind bent the steel rods that held down the LCVP boats; thus proving the force of the wind—strong enough to shift those big boats in their bolted down cradles. All hands that could be top side were ordered to do so with their life jackets on to ensure that no one would be trapped below deck if the ship sank. While topside, the waves were so bad that we had to hold on tight to the middle of the ship to avoid being washed overboard. At about 1200 hours, the Captain announced, "Secure all hatches, she is going to break in half any minute." I personally heard this, but again, nothing is said in the ship's log about the seriousness of this typhoon. As we later learned, a number of ships and men were lost in that typhoon, but none from the Cofer.

At 1815 hours, the typhoon had subsided and we got under way to Pusan, Korea. We later learned that 12 ships and craft ended up sinking, 222 were grounded, and 32 severely damaged. 36 people were killed with 47 missing and 100 seriously injured.

Saturday—October 13, 1945

Even though peace was signed, our Captain was cautious by setting condition "Able" below deck. This meant that all hands had to wear life jackets and be prepared for the possibility of hitting a Japanese mine and sinking quickly. In fact, a Japanese mine was seen floating in our path. One of our gunners exploded the mine with the Cofer's 20-mm gun. We were traveling alone from Okinawa toward Pusan, Korea.

Sunday—October 14, 1945

1630 hours, the Cofer arrived at the Pusan harbor entrance. Even though the war was over, we made a Japanese ship lead us through the harbor. When this Japanese ship was escorting us through the harbor, it hit a mine and sank. A local pilot then came aboard to steer the Cofer through the Korean minefield.

Monday—October 15, 1945

We tied up to pier #2 in Pusan, Korea. (Note, sometimes the ship's log listed this city as Pusan and other times as Fusan—I believe Fusan is correct.) Our ship, as we were told, was the flagship with directions to direct the Japanese to go back to Japan. The Japanese had dozens of ships in the harbor picking up Japanese that had been there for over 40 years to be taken back to Japan. It was shocking how many people they could stuff aboard these ships. I don't know how a fly could even have gotten onto those ships; they put so many people on each ship. All of their ships that I saw were named "Maru" something.

Tuesday—October 16, 1945

Today, the Cofer was still tied up to the dock in Fusan, Korea. Now our ship's log lists the city as Fusan, but at first it was listed as Pusan.

Today our ship did something that was unmilitary-like. We stole an Army jeep. A stack of jeeps were piled up in crates next to our ship. One night some of our people swung the boom around, picked up a jeep, and dumped it in the hole aboard ship. A few days later a few of my shipmates were riding around Fusan in a grey Navy painted jeep with fake numbers on the side.

There are two sad items that I remember happened while we were here. Once, a Japanese couple came up to the fan tail of our ship and the man said, "Japanese to have sex with Cofer sailor." There was an outdoor toilet at the end of the dock and she took on a number of sailors while her husband stood outside. The other unfortunate incident happened when the Koreans decided to hold a singing and dancing group of young girls to perform for all who wished to attend. It was in an area on the dock and I enjoyed the show, but some sailors were really rude toward them. This is the type of action that earned us the "Ugly Americans."

As I was serving as the Petty Officer in charge of the fan tail watch one morning, just before daylight, I remember when a really pretty Japanese girl came walking down the dock beside our ship. A sailor, who will remain anonymous, yelled something nasty at her as she walked past him, thinking she would not understand him. When she got near me she said, "That coffee you are drinking sure smells good." This girl was so nice and could speak perfect English. It turned out that she had graduated from the University of South Carolina. The sailor who had yelled at her stayed as far away from her as he could out of embarrassment.

I also vividly remember the time a white couple and their 12 year-old daughter visited our ship and several of us fed them. Our food was special to them. They, in turn, invited several of us back to their home for cookies and milk. Milk and cookies sounded absolutely great to us! They lived upstairs above a shop on the corner of a street. When we got upstairs, the wife started serving cookies and milk.

I asked, "Where did the milk come from?"

The wife answered, "Our cow."

Noticing that their place was very close to their neighbor's, I then asked, "Where do you keep your cow?"

Her reply was, "In the backyard!" We all rushed to the window to see her cow, and what a shock....it was a water buffalo lying in the mud and water. That was the end of our milk drinking in Korea.

October 17-22, 1945
Nothing happened during the next few days except for our usual scraping rust and painting.

Tuesday—October 23, 1945
Today, I was assigned the fan tail watch one night when an Army G.I. came up to me carrying a Japanese rifle and bayonet. He said, "Sailor, do you have anything you would trade me for this gun and bayonet?"

I replied, "I'd love to have it, but I don't have anything of value on me." He asked me for my flashlight and naturally, I jumped at his offer as it was a Navy-issued grey flashlight initialed U.S.N. The gun turned out to be a 7.7-mm short barrel, similar equal to our 30-30s. We all wanted Jap rifles for souvenirs. I kept it and was able to bring it home with me. Although it did have the serial number filed off, it still shoots well. At the time, the Japanese had to turn all of their rifles and pistols in to the Allied Forces. We were told that the Army had a whole warehouse full of Japanese rifles.

Wednesday—October 25, 1945
A large number of various U.S. Navy ships, merchant vessels, and Japanese ships were present today.

Thursday—October 26, 1945
The biggest happening today was the Captain's inspection topside and below deck.

Friday—October 27, 1945
Another captain's inspection was held today, two days in a row, which is most unusual. At 1900 hours, a Japanese ammunition supply dump exploded. It shook everybody and our ship quickly lit off the main engines so we would be ready to move if necessary. It ended up not being necessary.

Tuesday—October 30, 1945
One shipmate, J. Connor, left for home leave. This would not have happened before peace was signed.

Thursday—November 1, 1945
At 0610 hours, the USS Bridge (AF-1) reported striking a mine and was sinking. The Cofer was ordered to rush to assist. When we got to the USS Bridge, she was under tow by a Japanese tug boat. We followed them back to Fusan and stood by, supplying the USS Bridge with electricity and fresh water.

Friday—November 2, 1945
The Cofer was still in the outer harbor at Fusan, Korea, supplying steam, electricity and fresh water to the USS Bridge (AF-1). At 0947 hours, we got underway to follow the USS Bridge through the channel into the inner harbor. The USS Bridge got stuck on the bottom of the bay, which meant we had to wait until high tide came in for her to move. (Note: I have never seen tide rise as much as in Fusan. We would constantly be going up and down with the tide, always changing the links securing the ship to the dock.)

When we finally got back to Pier #2, a fire on the dock was noticed. The Cofer quickly sent fire personnel to assist.

Saturday—November 3, 1945
One LCVP boat left the Cofer with fire fighting equipment and damage-control parties to help combat another fire on Pier #1.

Monday—November 5, 1945
We moved back to our original Pier #1, which had been on fire two days ago.

Tuesday—November 6, 1945
The biggest activity today was transferring a number of shipmates to be discharged. More dull days were in store for us on the Cofer for most of November.

Tuesday—November 20, 1945
Finally, we were moving and off to Okinawa again, leaving at 0815 hours. At 1030 hours, we sighted a floating mine and our 20-mm guns exploded it.

Thursday—November 22, 1945
This morning we were joined en route to Okinawa with our sister ships, the USS Lloyd (APP-63) and the USS Kephart (APD-61), traveling in formation to Buckner Bay, Okinawa.

Friday—November 23, 1945
Anchored in Buckner Bay, Okinawa. We took on several Navy people to transfer to the U.S. We were all hoping that we would soon be heading home too.

Saturday—November 24, 1945
Still anchored. The Comtran's Division #103's Commander came aboard and presented our Captain H. C. McCleese with the Legion of Merit.

Sunday—November 25, 1945
Still at Buckner Bay. We received approximately 130 Navy personnel aboard for transportation to the U.S. mainland. This meant that we would soon be on our way home!

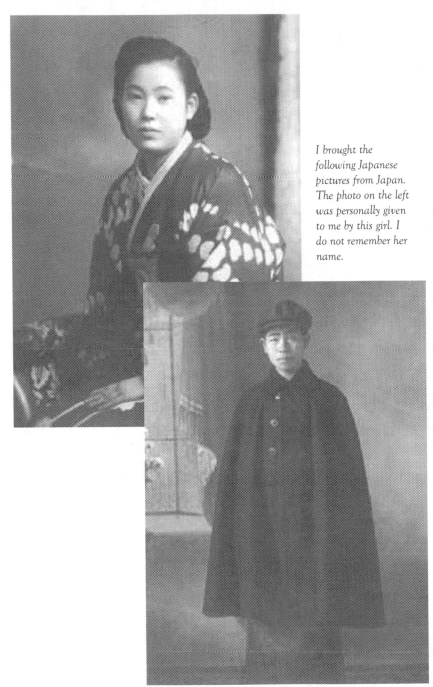

I brought the following Japanese pictures from Japan. The photo on the left was personally given to me by this girl. I do not remember her name.

This is a picture of a supposed
Japanese movie star.

James Richard Snellen

Partially sunken warship in the Okinawa harbor.

The Japanese printed this Japanese occupational money while occupying the Philippines. Note "PI" on the top and bottom for the Philippine Islands.

James Richard Snellen

*Japanese Prisoners of
War–Philippines 1944*

Wakayama, Japan—this picture was taken from the Cofer of a small Japanese boat as we entered the harbor on September 11, 1945. Seventeen of us went ashore that first night to set up a radio station. Below: Photo of a Japanese truck taken in the Philippines.

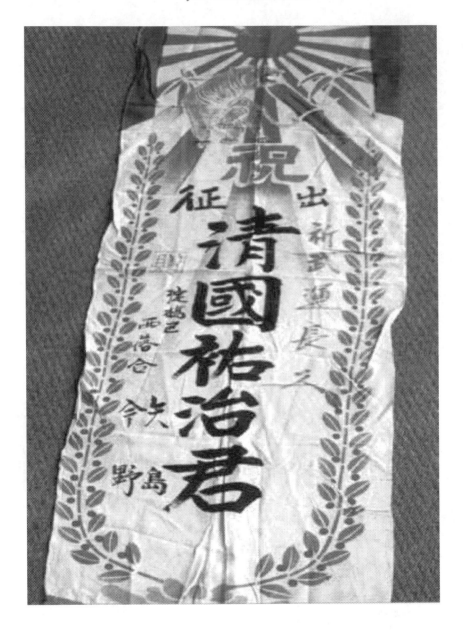

Japanese banner reportedly displayed during celebrations on the Philippine Islands.

23 SEPTEMBER 1945.

TO: THE COMMANDING OFFICER.

SIR:

THE BRITISH AND AMERICAN EX-PRISONERS OF WAR TRANSPORTED ON THIS SHIP FROM NAGASAKI WISH RESPECTFULLY TO CONVEY THEIR GRATEFUL THANKS AND APPRECIATION TO THE SHIP'S OFFICERS AND COMPANY FOR THE EFFICIENCY, COURTESY, AND KINDNESS SHOWN TO THEM ON THIS TRIP.

ONLY MEN WHO HAVE BEEN AWAY FROM THEIR HOMES FOR LONG PERIODS, AS YOU HAVE AND WE HAVE, CAN REALIZE HOW MUCH THIS TRIP HAS MEANT TO US.

WE WISH YOU ALL GOOD LUCK AND A SPEEDY RETURN TO THE UNITED STATES.

THE BRITISH AND AMERICAN EX-PRISONERS OF WAR.

Above: This is a thank you letter written to our Commanding Officer from the British POWs that we evacuated from Japan. Below: American soldiers and local young people holding white peace flags.

Top: Japanese money I received in Japan in September 1945.
Below: Someone aboard the Cofer took this picture as we were entering the Wakayama harbor.

PRIVATE CODE,

Compiled by

NAGASAKI YOKO, INC.,

(NAGASAKI, JAPAN)
—*from*—

SUPPLEMENT
—*to*—

BENTLEY'S COMPLETE PHRASE CODE

APRIL, 1938

This is the code book that I picked up while in Nagasaki, Japan. It was, no doubt, hot with radiation, but we were not aware of the danger back then. On the right: I am presenting this book at our Cofer reunion

10

Monday—November 26, 1945
At 0801 hours, they lit off the Cofer's main engines and by 0912 hours, we were underway for Pearl Harbor, Hawaii in company with three of our sister ships, the USS Newman (APD-59), the USS Kephart (APD-61), and the USS Lloyd (APD-63)—the commanding ship. We were all thrilled to be headed back to the States!

Tuesday—November 27, 1945
Our crew had taken old, cut up Army parachutes to make a return flag to fly from the mast of our ship to the fantail. This enormous flag flapped in the wind all the way back to the States.

While en route for Hawaii, we dropped the jeep that we had stolen in Fusan, Korea into the sea. We had to. It was an Army jeep that had been painted Navy gray with a fake serial number on it.

An American jeep, very similar to the one our ship "stole" before it was painted Navy gray with false serial numbers to its sides.

Monday—December 3, 1945
The Cofer went alongside the USS Kephart to exchange movies and mail. I cannot remember why the mail was exchanged, unless one of us had gotten the other's mail by mistake back in Buckner Bay.

Friday—December 7, 1945
Today was the anniversary of Pearl Harbor Day—still at sea, steaming toward Pearl Harbor.

Saturday—December 8, 1945
After thirteen days of sailing, we finally arrived at the Pearl Harbor entrance channel at 1654 hours. The Cofer tied up to the USS Kephart (APD-61).

Sunday—December 9, 1945
20 men were received aboard for transportation to the mainland. Later in the day, we had one full day of liberty in Pearl Harbor. As I often look back, I thought we had had three or four days of liberty, but the ship's log only lists one day's leave. Anyway, we really let our hair down.

This was a wonderful day—almost like suddenly being released from jail. For one year and three months of sleeping aboard a ship, usually expecting anything at any moment, and then suddenly arriving at such a fun place, being free to do whatever you desired was like leaving hell and arriving in heaven. I spent most of my time ashore on Waikiki Beach and the Royal Hawaiian Hotel. Some forty years later, I returned to Hawaii and I had to see this hotel. It still looked great, but unless I was wrong, it originally had been facing the beach. Now a larger hotel has been built between it and the beach.

After being at sea for more than a year in horrible war time, Honolulu was another world to us.

Monday—December 10, 1945
At 1540 hours, we cast off all lines and set course for San Diego. What a happy bunch we were!

Tuesday—December 11, 1945
At sea all day heading for San Diego.

Saturday—December 15, 1945
Still heading for San Diego. We were now cruising at 17 knots. We were in a hurry to get home!

Sunday—December 16, 1945

At 1358 hours, we finally arrived in the San Diego harbor. Several Cofer shipmates transferred ashore to San Diego. At first we weren't going to be allowed to go ashore at all until a day or two after arrival. One sailor actually jumped overboard that night, trying to swim ashore—desperate to be back at home after being out to sea for 18 months. He was drunk, and they had to fish him out.

Monday—December 17, 1945

Our Captain Herbert C. McLeese was relieved of his command and Lt. James R. Morrow, regular Navy, replaced Captain McLeese. Our own Lt. W. C. Meredith was transferred to take command of the USS Newman (APD-59) and Lt. S. W. (Will) Hahn was promoted to Executive Officer of the Cofer to replace Lt. Meredith.

Tuesday—December 18, 1945

Moored in berth #24 at the Navy Repair Base in San Diego, California. At 1845 hours, sixteen additional men reported aboard for duty.

Wednesday—December 19, 1945

At 1700 hours, a number of our shipmates were transferred ashore for separation. Two of our LCVP boat crew members were transferred, and I knew I would miss them. Especially sad for me was the transfer of Walter Whitaker, our LCVP #2's Coxswain. He was a true friend and a person for whom I have so much respect for. When we first met in Ft. Pierce in May of 1944, I was only 17 years-old, and he started calling me "The Kid." After the war, we stayed in close contact as he and his wife, Maxine, visited my family more than once. Also, he was so supportive of our Cofer reunions which were started in 1987.

Thursday—December 20, 1945

Today, the ships' log lists several of our shipmates being AWOL, and this was understandable after being in the South Pacific under such horrible conditions for more than a year. They, of course, received minor punishments according to the hours they were AWOL.

Friday—December 21, 1945

We were still moored alongside the USS Newman (APD-59) today. The Newman's new captain was our former Executive Officer Lt. Walter Meredith.

Sunday—December 23, 1945
One of my friends, Everett Darling, was transferred ashore for discharge from the Navy. (In our Cofer Association, Everett, or "Ev" for short, became the financial person for our association and still is in 2007. He was a Yeoman, 2nd Class, aboard the Cofer.)

Monday—December 24, 1945
Today was Christmas Eve and this was our greatest Christmas to look forward to. We were all given a three day leave. Suddenly, similar to Honolulu, I felt free again. Several of my shipmates and I checked into the Saint James Hotel in San Diego, California. We had a fun time! I have included one picture of two other Gunner's Mates (Ira Fouts and Don Mericle) and myself in San Diego. We really let our hair down.

My wife, Dorothy, and I went back to San Diego when I was working in Los Angeles in 1981 and I had to see if the old St. James Hotel was still there. It was, and when seeing it from the outside, I was so pleased. But what a shock I received when I entered the hotel's front door! Sitting all around inside the lobby were what appeared to be street people. I backed out, but was still pleased to again see the hotel where we had so much fun in December of 1945.

Our first night back in the States-December 24, 1946 in San Diego, California. (Left to right) Don Mericle, Jim Snellen, and Ira Fouts.

Tuesday—December 25, 1945
On Christmas Day, the Cofer was still moored alongside the USS Newman (APD-59). Another one of our shipmates, who reportedly had too much to drink, jumped overboard and tried to swim ashore. Our LCVP boat picked him up and no charges were filed.

Wednesday—December 26, 1945
At 0600 hours, we started to leave to get underway for Balboa in the Panama Canal Zone. Our speeds were up to 17 knots and we were, again, in a hurry.

Thursday—December 27, 1945
Four shipmates got into a fight while underway. The Captain held mast and assigned each 25 hours of extra duty.

Sunday—December 30, 1945
Still cruising toward the Panama Canal.

Monday—December 31, 1945
Today was a repeat to the past five days. We were excited about getting to visit Panama City again. It was a wonderful liberty city for sailors.

Tuesday—January 1, 1946
We were finally approaching the entrance of the Panama Canal Channel. At 1645 hours, we stopped and tied up to Pier #2 in Balboa, Panama. Four officers and six Army, Marine, and Navy men came aboard for transportation to the East Coast of the United States. I was quite disappointed, as we were only given one night of liberty in Panama City. Previously, we had been given several nights of liberty before leaving for the South Pacific—but not this time.

Thursday—January 3, 1946
At 2035 hours, we started to move toward the entrance of the canal locks following the USS Newman (APD-59).

Friday—January 4, 1946
We cleared the locks of the canal and headed east. Some problem developed with the steering and the Cofer reportedly had to go to AFT steering. When using the AFT steering, the pilots can take over from below deck if the steering failed. (This happened when the bridge of the USS Liddle (APD-60) was hit by a suicide Japanese plane. Most of the bridge was blown away, so the AFT steering took over

after a period of time.)

For the next five days we were steaming from the Panama Canal toward the Brooklyn Navy Yard in Brooklyn, New York. Along the way, much was being done to prepare the Cofer for arrival at the Brooklyn Navy yard.

I was the Gunner's Mate in charge of the small arms locker that held rifles and other small arms. When in the South Pacific, we often picked up American pilots who had been shot down or had to bail out of their planes. They would always have a 45-mm pistol strapped to their side. When these pilots boarded the Cofer, they had to turn over their pistols, which quickly went into the Cofer's small arms locker. When we were off the coast of Cuba, I went to my Gunnery Officer, Scotty Parrish, and asked what I should do with the seven or eight 45-mm pistols that were in the small arms locker, not listed as Cofer property. Scotty said, "I don't care what you do with them, but make sure they are not in that locker when we arrive in New York." I was afraid to try to keep them or give them away to other shipmates, so I dropped all seven or eight overboard. As it turned out, I could have gotten away with taking all of these guns off the ship and home with me. I've often regretted tossing them into the ocean.

Wednesday—January 9, 1946
The Cofer tied up at the Navy pier in Sandy Hook Bay, New Jersey and unloaded all ammunitions. We had everything from 5-inch shells down to 30-caliber shells. I assume our depth charges were taken off also. At 1537 hours, two pilots came aboard to steer us into the docks at the Brooklyn Navy Yards in New York. Later, all temporary personnel that we had picked up in San Diego and Panama departed the Cofer.

Friday—January 11, 1946
I cannot remember exactly which day the majority of us were given leave to return home, so I will guess. All I remember is how wonderful it was, after being away for 16 months, to be home again in Kentucky.

My older brother, Herbert, Jr., who had earlier been discharged from the Air Force, really showed me around. I dated several girls and thought I was hot stuff. I hated to return to New York to go back to sea again in the middle of the winter. We had no heat on the ship and it was cold!

Friday—January 25, 1946
A pilot came aboard and shifted the Cofer to a dry dock in the Brooklyn Navy Yard to check and paint the belly side.

Monday—January 28, 1946
The Cofer spent the day in the dry dock hooked up to freshwater and electricity. Later today we received a number of men aboard for temporary duty.

Tuesday—January 29, 1946
Today some Cofer sailors who had been AWOL received their sentences. The sentences would mostly depend upon how long they had been AWOL and how serious of a time they had been gone. For example, if the ship was ready to sail, this was the worst time to be AWOL! To serve out their sentence, men usually had to work extra hours, lose some of their liberty, or be docked pay. Most anything could have been charged to them. I personally was never on captain's mast. Not many men in the Navy could say that!

We received 10 additional men for temporary duty today.

Friday—February 1, 1946
Still in dry dock. Two shipmates returned for duty from the Brooklyn Navy hospital.

Saturday—February 2, 1946
While the Cofer was still in dry dock being worked on, we had free time in New York City once again. At the beginning of my service, I had met a beautiful, nice girl from Ozone Park. Now I used my leave time to go on several dates with her. We had written back and forth throughout the entire time that I had been in the South Pacific. We thought that we were serious, but both of us were too young.

February 3-4, 1946
Still in dry dock.

Tuesday—February 5, 1946
A fire broke out in the blower's room due to a welder's spark while repairs were being made to the Cofer. The damage turned out to only be minor.

Wednesday—February 6, 1946
Finally, we prepared to leave the dry dock. Water was pumped in and we were moved out by a side wench and then moored alongside the USS Kephart (APD-59).

Thursday—February 7, 1946
Still moored alongside the USS Kephart. At 1300 hours, several of my friends were transferred to the recruiting station for discharge. It was always bittersweet to see your friends leave for discharge. The Navy had a formula that counted your age, time in service, and sea duty that qualified you for discharge. I was only six months past my nineteenth birthday and I continuously wondered when I would be eligible for discharge.

Friday—February 8, 1946
For me, today was a day to remember. At 1220 hours, I was transferred to the U.S. Naval hospital in Brooklyn, New York for treatment of a serious sore throat. They sent all of my records with me in case I did not return before the Cofer received orders to leave. I was really hoping to not go back to sea, at least for a while. We had no heat on the ship, which was probably the cause of my sore throat. The Navy classified my problem as "monopolist diagnostic infection." They put me on penicillin and I did not enjoy those shots. After all that we had gone through in the Pacific, getting regular shots bothered me even more.

Saturday—February 9, 1946
I was in the hospital.

Thursday—February 14, 1946
I was still in the hospital.
        Today, the Captain held captain's mast and issued mild punishments to those charged.

Friday—February 15, 1946
Two other captain's masts were held today on the Cofer. New York was just too much fun—too many sailors were getting into trouble.

Thursday—February 21, 1946
I returned to the Cofer today from the Brooklyn Navy Hospital. I was hoping not to go back to sea because it was not comfortable aboard the cold ship, especially when the seas were rough.

Friday—February 22, 1946
Still moored in Berth #4 within the naval shipyards in Brooklyn, New York taking on fresh water, steam and electricity.

Saturday—February 23, 1946
Almost a ditto of yesterday. Present today were various merchant ships and one special to us—the U.S.S. Montpelier (CL-57). The Montpelier was with us throughout the Borneo operations and our trips to Okinawa, Japan and Korea. She was like a sister ship to us.

Wednesday—February 27, 1946
Still moored in the naval yard. We were still wondering where we would go next.

Sunday—March 3, 1946
The only excitement on ship today was that we received water and electricity from the shore.
    I was really missing my closest friend, William E. Flippo, this time in New York. Flippo never returned to active duty after his accident on June 14 , 1945.

Monday—March 4, 1946
As before, we were present for muster and then free until the next morning unless assigned a special project aboard ship. Only a skeleton crew was required on board, so we were living it up in New York City. The GIs were loved by all now that World War II was finally over. No anti-war activity was going on—that didn't happen until the Vietnam War. Back then, you could go into a restaurant or a bar somewhere and someone would grab your check and treat you to drinks. You could stand beside the road and someone would almost always offer you a ride. No words can truly justify the appreciation that people had for military men.

Thursday—March 7, 1946
The Cofer took on water, steam, and electricity from shore. One shipmate returned aboard one hour and fifteen minutes late. I will not mention his name.

Friday—March 8, 1946
There were a number of ships in view of us and one special to us was the battleship USS North Carolina (BB-55). This was a beautiful sight, especially compared to our small APD.

Saturday—March 9, 1946
Moored as before. At 1019 hours, both the USS Barrett (PC-109) and also the USS Keats (DE-278), which had been attached to the Cofer, cast off lines.

Wednesday—March 13, 1946

Today, as every Wednesday and Saturday, we were served the traditional Navy cornbread and beans again. This is a Navy tradition, apparently from the first years of the Navy's creation. The beans were always a little red, so I assume catsup was probably mixed in. The cornbread was always cut into two-inch squares. None of us ever looked forward to Wednesday or Saturday breakfasts.

Talking about food...I will go back to our time in the South Pacific. Except for sheep or maybe goat meat, we never had fresh meat. These sheep or goats came aboard whole and skinned minus the head and feet from Australia. Our regular food consisted of dried milk, canned dried eggs, Spam (one of my favorites, even now), and dehydrated potatoes, and canned chipped beef which they would mix with gravy and put over toast. They had a name for this that I will not mention.

Thursday—March 14, 1946

Still moored in the Brooklyn Navy Yard, but it was a great day for several close friends including P.J. Adams, Charles Teague, Art Conn, and Ed Przybyl. They were among several men transferred off the Cofer for discharge from the Navy. You had to have so many points to be qualified for a discharge. It was your time in service plus your age. (I had turned 19 in September and my age did not earn me many points). The number of months at sea also played a part. I certainly missed those guys.

Friday—March 15, 1946

A tug boat came alongside to move the USS Keats (DE-178) from our starboard side. They goofed up by not removing the gangway, which in turn damaged our watertight hatch. Five hours later, workmen had repaired the damage.

Saturday—March 16, 1946

Two men reported aboard after being AWOL. At 0820 hours, Yard Pilot Kelley and Channel Pilot J. B. Brown came aboard. After we had loaded 41,000 gallons of fuel, we got underway proceeding out of the New York Naval Shipyard. We were en route to Jacksonville, Florida to join the Navy's "Mothball Fleet." They called this Navy base in Green Cove Springs the "Mothball Fleet" because we were preparing to seal the guns and ship for possible future use. The reason for selecting Green Cove Springs for this was the St. John's River was a fresh water river flowing hundreds of miles north from South Florida. Getting the ships into freshwater prevented further rust, or at least less rusting than if the ship were left in salt water.

Sunday—March 17, 1946
Cruising at 16 knots, heading south toward Jacksonville, Florida.

Monday—March 18, 1946
At 1530 hours, we passed Florida's St. John's Lighthouse on our starboard side. 20 minutes later, Pilot L.T. Erwin came aboard and we proceeded at various channel speeds entering the St. John's River and St. John's River Channel. At 1750 hours, we came alongside the USS Yahara (AOG-37) at Commodore's Point, in Jacksonville, Florida and moored on the starboard side of the USS Yahara. At 1807 hours, we secured from sea detail and set in-port watch.

Tuesday—March 19, 1946
Today the Cofer was still moored to the USS Yahara (AOG-37) at the naval receiving docks in Jacksonville, Florida. At 1405 hours, pilot J.S. Peck came aboard and we untied from the pier at Jacksonville to get underway for Green Cove Springs, conforming to the St. John's River speeds. Half an hour later the pilot left the ship and we dropped anchor in three fathoms of water—mud bottom.

Mothball fleet of decommissioned World War II warships at
Green Cove Springs, Florida in 1946. The Cofer is seen in the middle—APD-62.

11

Wednesday—March 20, 1946
We were finally anchored in the St. John's River at Green Cover Springs, Florida. There were about 600 ships present from the U.S. 16th fleet.

Thursday—March 21, 1946
On this day, Officer Doug Demarest transferred to the Naval Hospital with pneumonia. A number of men were called to captain's mast today due to earlier absences without leave. Some were AWOL for one day, others for five days. It seemed that many of us, including me, hated to leave New York and head back to sea after one and a half years aboard the Cofer in the South Pacific. It was not easy to always be on time and never make a mistake (or at least enough to be reported wrong by Navy rules).

While in the South Pacific, I did do something wrong, however. We were underway one Sunday morning when Mr. McClendon (that is Ensign Edwin J. McClendon, my boat officer, who we always referred to our officers as "Mr.") piped me top side. He was holding a paint bucket and the paint brush and he said, "Be careful. This is the last paint brush aboard ship." He wanted me to touch up something on the outside of one of the LCVP boats. The sea was calm that day, yet the Cofer was rolling from side to side. So, I got the bright idea to set the bucket of paint next to the edge of the ship with the brush on top. When the Cofer rolled left, I touched the paint can with my foot just enough to send the brush and paint flying over board. Mr. McClendon took his white hat off and slammed it on the deck, using some strong words. He knew, however, that he could not say that it wasn't an accident.

Many, many years later at our Cofer reunion in Canton, Ohio, my wife Dorothy (Dot) and I had breakfast with Mr. McClendon (now Dr. McClendon, Ph. D.). I remember telling him, "Mac, I have a confession to make. Something has bothered me all these years...I must tell you about that bucket of paint and paint brush..." He looked at me with his beady eyes, as if he could eat me alive. (I know he, too, thought it was funny. But he would not let on.) Ruby McClendon, his wife, thought it was hilarious. He said the Captain had wanted to court martial me because of the paint all down the Cofer. He later told this story many times at our next reunions. But who ever heard of the Navy only having one paint brush? We chipped and painted every single day while in port or anchored.

Friday—March 22, 1946
This was a day for us to become accustomed to being anchored in the middle of the river in the U.S. In the South Pacific, we were always anchored somewhere at sea if we were not underway. But, to be anchored in a river and to be at home was something! The new Captain was busy holding captain's mast for those doing (or failing to do) something to break Navy rules.

Saturday—March 23, 1946
Another dull day. By now, many of our crew members had been discharged, so we were operational at half strength.

Wednesday—March 28, 1945
We moved and tied up with four other APDs when a storm hit and the anchors were dragged. Our ship then untied and anchored separately to ride out the storm. To do so, we had to start two engines as if getting ready for sea detail. By this time, we were all accustomed to the ship's constant rocking and rolling so no one would get seasick. Sometimes if we had been in port for a while and then got underway in rough weather, I would get a little dizzy, but I can only remember one time that I had gotten seasick at the beginning of my duty.

Thursday—March 29, 1946
The Cofer anchored again and tied up alongside the USS Belet (APD-10), USS Hollis (APD-86), USS Frament (APD-77), and USS (YTL-295). The Hollis started furnishing us electricity from her generator.

At first all 600 ships were anchored in the St. John's River. But after docks were built, they were moved from anchorage to be tied to the docks. I have often wondered about sewage from these 600 sea-going war ships.

Monday—April 1, 1946
Still anchored at Green Cove Springs, Florida. My new promotion to Gunner's Mate 3rd Class gave me more authority aboard ship. I was ordered to pick up sailors from our ship who had been picked up for misbehavior (usually in Jacksonville, 28 miles to the north)—usually more often than not, due to excessive drinking. They were held by the shore patrol in downtown Green Cove Springs at the brig. I had to strap a 45 pistol on my hip, often wondering what would have

happened if I had been forced to use my gun.

Tuesday—April 2, 1946
Nothing much happened today except one good friend was AWOL, but only by four hours over his leave.

Wednesday—April 3, 1946
Still anchored at Green Cove Springs. We received fresh water and electricity from the USS Hollis (APD-86). By mid-morning, a number of Cofer shipmates were transferred to the local hanger with bags to be discharged. One boat crew friend of mine, A. Kolthoff, was among those leaving the ship. It was dull carrying out the daily tasks of preparing the ship for "moth balling."

Thursday—April 4, 1946
I was one of the youngest still left aboard because most of the older sailors, unless they were regular Navy, had already left the ship for discharge. The regular Navy men had mostly joined the Navy before the war or were Annapolis, Maryland graduates. The rest of us were classified as Navy Reserves. As I mentioned earlier, in order to be discharged from the Navy Reserves, a man had to earn enough points. I had turned 19 six months earlier and April marked my completion of two years of service. You got one point for your age and half a point for each month at sea (or maybe it was the other way around). Regardless, I did not think I would ever get discharged.

Since I was a right arm gunner's mate, I was the one often chosen to take a 45-mm pistol strapped to my side, have one of our boats take me to the dock, and then go to the temporary brig and pick up sailors from the Cofer and bring them back to the ship. Usually the prisoners were being charged with disorderly conduct in Jacksonville or Green Cove Springs. It always seemed unfair (to me, at least) to bring them back under armed guard. I was always afraid one would try to escape—then what would I have done?

Saturday—April 6, 1946
We were anchored at the east end of the drawbridge in the St. John's River. Something of personal concern to me was the fact that my former officer, Lt. J.G. McClendon, was sent to the Jacksonville Naval Hospital for treatment. He had been my boat officer until the war ended.

Monday—April 8, 1946
About the only activity today that was five Cofer shipmates were AWOL.

Saturday—April 13, 1946
Counting the days until I would hopefully be discharged.

Sunday—April 14, 1946
The only activity today was that one of the recent AWOL shipmates was delivered aboard under armed guard from the Shore Patrol Headquarters.

Monday—April 15, 1946
Today consisted of the usual dull work day with a captain's mast held for five shipmates who had been AWOL. They were punished with 77 hours of extra duty. It was silly for these guys to be getting into trouble with such a short time left before being discharged.

Wednesday—April 24, 1946
Several men transferred today for discharge. Lt. J. R. Morrow, a new commanding officer, took over the Cofer today from regular Navy.

Thursday—April 25, 1946
All aboard would take every leave possible to go ashore to just get away from the ship. One day several of us even rented a car for fun and drove down to a big lake and got stuck in the sand. The more we spun the rear wheels, the deeper the wheels would go into the sand. Finally, some local people brought boards and helped us get out. We learned what not to do in loose sand!

Monday—April 29, 1946
Odd as it seems, several men reported aboard for duty today. It seems unusual to receive new men aboard at this time.

Friday—May 3, 1946
Lt. Commander W. J. McNulty, Commander of the USS Hoping (APD-51), replaced our commanding officer J.R. Morrow.

Saturday—May 4, 1946
We were still anchored in the middle of the St. John's River along with more than 600 sea-going war ships. Today I studied the depth of the river. All reports that I have heard said that the river was 30 fathoms deep and our ship had out 60 fathoms of anchor chain. I understand a fathom is six feet. So the river at our anchor point supposedly was 90 feet deep. I have been told that they had to dredge the St. John's River to permit these sea-going war ships to come 28 miles

down river from Jacksonville.

Monday—May 6, 1946
One of the nicest officers, Lt. Philip Albert, left the ship for Great Lakes for discharge. Many years later, my wife, Dot, and I later met Mrs. Albert over an especially nice lunch at her Country Club here in Jacksonville.

Tuesday—May 7, 1946
Most of today was the usual work of preparing the ship for her final preparation to be a mothball ship. Four years later, the Korean War started and the Cofer was called to duty once more. Back when we were doing duty in Fusan, Korea, I would write home to friends and family and many of them mentioned that they had never heard of Korea before. The Korean War, unfortunately, made everyone in the United States very aware of where Korea was on the map.

Thursday—May 9, 1946
Our biggest activity today was that another shipmate reported aboard for duty. To me, this is odd because by this time, the sealing of the ship for the decommissioning to join the Mothball Fleet was almost complete.

Friday—May 10, 1946
Two more new shipmates reported for duty.

Wednesday—May 15, 1946
WHAT A BIG DAY FOR ME! Finally, I was able to leave the Cofer for discharge at the Great Lakes Naval Training Center in Great Lakes, Illinois. The other boat crew members who also left with me to be discharged were Johnny Ehling, Joe Wajerski, C.D. Mead, and our boat officer Edwin D. McClendon. McClendon went to Memphis; Mead to Norman, Oklahoma; Wajerski, Ehling and I went to Great Lakes.

Thursday—May 16, 1946
Today Joe Wajerski, John Ehling and I traveled from Green Cove Springs, Florida to Great Lakes. After all these years I can not even remember how we traveled to Great Lakes, but it had to have been by train. Back then it seemed that this was the only way the military traveled in the States, unless it was urgent; then they would fly you. I suspect it took us two days to get to Great Lakes.

Saturday—May 18 and 19, 1946
I was officially discharged from the Navy.

Monday—May 20, 1946
It took me about one day to get back to my hometown in Kentucky.

Each tiny speck in the St. John's River represents a sea-going warship. There were a total of 620 ships tied up to the docks at Green Cove Springs.

Afterwords

When I arrived in Louisville, Kentucky, school was out for the summer of 1946. Before I left, I had been so anxious to get into the service that I had quit in my third year of high school to join the Navy.

I started to work at American-Standard in Louisville, which was the same place my father had worked for all of his working life. It was the first and only company he had ever worked for. I only worked there for a few weeks because it was a hard, tough job. I later started working at a big hardware store as a salesman in training while the government supplemented my salary. While there, I learned much about meeting people and selling products. After a period of time, I became restless and then returned to high school in Brandenburg, Kentucky, because I realized how dumb it was for me to drop out of high school.

While at high school, I started dating my typing teacher. She was only one year older than me, which should not have been a problem because I was a returning veteran. But her brother, who was a local attorney, disagreed. So she broke off our friendship. As I write this today, I recently learned that she has passed away due to cancer.

I was accepted at the University of Louisville under the GI Bill where the government would pay all expenses for one year more than my length of time in the Navy. So, because I had already had one year of high school paid by the government, I could have gone for two full years at the University of Louisville at the government's expense. But, I was restless. Because of what I had been through in the South Pacific, I felt like an old man compared to those young college kids. I later switched to night school and then got a job and worked during the day.

On the 4th of July in 1947, I met my wife to be, Dorothy Stocker, on a blind date. She was engaged to another sailor, but on that day, he was in the hospital for something he had picked up in the South Pacific. And so I guess it was just a coincidental meeting that we went out on the 4th of July. We really had a lot of fun that day and she finally broke it off with the other guy. That's when I decided it was best for me to get away. Dorothy's family owned a grocery store and a filling station and they had so much more than my family, who was rich in love and family, but we didn't have much else. I knew I could not offer her the lifestyle she was accustomed to.

I quit my hardware store job and re-enlisted, but this time in the U.S. Air Force. I requested foreign service duty, and they immediately gave me an Air

Force uniform and put me to work. But you won't believe where they assigned me—Godman Air Force Base at Fort Knox, Kentucky. So my original thinking that it would be best for me to leave Kentucky was not in the cards. I was now located closer to Dorothy than I had been in Louisville!

Soon after arriving at Ft. Knox, I was selected to go to an office administration school at Middletown Air Depot in Middletown, Pennsylvania (which today is now the Harrisburg International Airport). I went to school for approximately three months and then was transferred back for duty at Fort Knox. As a Corporal in the Air Force, I was assigned to work in the administration office in charge of the enlisted men's records. At my finger tips, I had everything the Air Force knew about a group of about 300 enlisted men at the base.

Soon I was advised that I had the second highest IQ of any enlisted man assigned to that base. It was suggested that I take a test to be admitted to Officer's Candidate School. I agreed to go for it. When we received our instructions for the test, we were told that any unanswered questions would be counted against you. But when the test was concluded, the test administrators came back and said that actually any unanswered questions would NOT have been counted against you. I could not believe this! I failed. My score was 108 and I needed a 115 to pass. They told me that I could come back and re-take the test after six weeks.

That was it. I decided then and there that I wanted out of the service. I finally felt that I had grown up. Before, I had been a confused 19 year-old. Even though I was not a hero in the South Pacific, I had seen a lot. I was now ready to start a new life.

My role in the administration office gave me access to all enlisted men's records and I knew some who had requested a discharge. The one person that I can still remember had put in a request for a "hardship discharge" from Dayton, Ohio. His request had been denied all because his wife had just purchased a new refrigerator. They had several children and, no doubt, he was needed at home.

I told my warrant officer that I was going to apply for a discharge. At that time, President Truman was letting men out of the service to work on family farms if needed badly enough. My mother and dad had just purchased an old farm in Meade County, Kentucky that did not even have electricity or indoor plumbing. So, when I put my discharge request together after thoroughly studying all of the many other requests, I wrote a real tear jerker—I kid you not! My officer had earlier told me, "You little 'so and so'. You don't have a Chinaman's chance of getting out." But as he read my request, I could see the blood drain from his face. It was policy—he had to sign it.

So six weeks and two days later, I was again a civilian. I later found out that the person from the Red Cross who had been sent to investigate my request and the state of my family's farm had been one of my high school teachers in Meade County. The cards, no doubt, were strongly in my favor this time.

Soon after I received an honorable Air Force discharge, Dorothy and I were married on her 20th birthday—February 12, 1949. On July 10, 1951, Vicki, our only daughter, was born. She was and has always been so special to us.

After leaving the service, I began working for a variety of manufacturing companies, mostly in the heating and air conditioning field. Later, I moved to marketing and became a zone sales manager for General Motors and American Standard for 10 years. I've worked in every state in the continental United States and Hawaii, except Montana and Wyoming.

In 1998, I was able to retire and move to Fruit Cove, Florida. At the time, I never dreamed that I'd be living within 15 miles of the place where the Cofer had been decommissioned! Every time I cross the bridge over the St. John's River, I can picture myself being aboard the Cofer. Green Cove Springs used to be a Navy base, and I golf down there now once a week on the old Navy golf course. It always brings back memories.

Our yearly Cofer reunions began when a brother of a sailor who was lost on a ship that sunk in the Brunei Bay by the name of Schaffer from Shepardsville, Kentucky, wrote to Dear Abby and asked if she would put out a notice asking if anyone knew anything about his ship sinking. In Brunei Bay, the Cofer had picked up and we had buried some casualties from that area, but we didn't find Schaffer's body. Someone from our ship wrote to him and began to gather all of us for a reunion. 62 years later, our association has now had 17 annual reunions since 1987.

Part of my role as the Cofer's historian is to keep in contact with all of my shipmates whom we have been able to locate. Many whom have passed away have died from different forms of cancer. No doubt, the different forms of cancer could have been caused by exposure to radiation in Nagasaki, Japan on August 9, 1945.

At our reunion in Williamsburg, Virginia in 1996, we had a General from the Philippines who worked in the Philippine embassy in Washington, D.C. join us. He and his wife talked with our group and presented each of us with a Philippine liberation medal. He had been captured and was in the Bataan Death March. This was a war crime committed by the Japanese against prisoners of war in 1942 after the Battle of Bataan. That was one of the saddest stories I've ever heard someone tell.

Today, I am the only one of the four of our boat crew members still living. Walter Whitaker, our Coxswain, just died a few years ago. We were good friends until his death and his wife was also a very good friend of ours until her death.

Our Engineer, Gilbert Crippen, was electrocuted while working as an electrician. William Flippo, our other Gunner, named his first son after me. He died in 1986 at his home in Mississippi.

For my time in the service, I received two bronze star medals, a combat action ribbon, a China service medal, American campaign medal, Asiatic-Pacific campaign medal with 8 stars, a Navy commendation medal, and a World War II victory metal.

After receiving 8 battle stars, the Cofer was decommissioned in 1947 and berthed at Green Cove Springs, Florida and she was sold on March 5, 1968. Of all of the 270 DE/APD Class ships, there were only 6 other ships receiving more battle stars than the USS Cofer.

I remember so many details of my Navy service...there are many things that I'd rather forget. But for me, it has been a wonderful life.

I owe so much to so many.

James Snellen at home in 2007.

JAMES R. SNELLEN

LOUISVILLE, KY 1946

Rate / Rank
GM3

Service Branch
USNR

Service Dates
4/1944 - 6/1946

Born
9/27/1926
VALLEY STATION, KY

NAVY LOG

SIGNIFICANT DUTY STATIONS

- NTS GREAT LAKES, IL * AMPHIB LCVP BOAT TRAINING, FORT PIERCE, FL
- USS COFER DE-208 / APD-62
- SOUTH PACIFIC INVASIONS
- PHILIPPINES * BORNEO
- OKINAWA & NAGASAKI, JAPAN

SIGNIFICANT AWARDS

- BRONZE STAR MEDAL (2) * NAVY COMMENDATION MEDAL
- COMBAT ACTION RIBBON * CHINA SERVICE MEDAL
- AMERICAN CAMPAIGN MEDAL
- ASIATIC-PACIFIC CAMPAIGN MEDAL W/8 STARS
- WORLD WAR II VICTORY MEDAL

My list of commemorations during my service aboard the Cofer (APD-62).

Above: My Navy insignia and medals of honor.

Right: Jim Snellen– US Air Force in 1947. I left the U.S. Air Force as a Corporal after 11 months. President Truman was allowing honorable discharge if needed on the family farm.

I reenlisted in the 11th Air Force, stationed at Godman Field, Ft. Knox, Kentucky. It didn't take long from me to realize that was a mistake!

A few of my fellow whipmates and I returned to Green Cove Springs in April of 2006 for our Cofer reunion. Jim Snellen (left), Don Mericle, Scotty Parrish, and Walter Maki. We are holding a map of all the ships which were once at Green Cove Springs.

Top: 2006 San Antonio Reunion—(left to right) Edwin J. McClendon, Jim Snellen, Captain Alvin P. Chester, and Scotty Parish.

Left: Captain Chester at our San Antonio reunion.

135

Top: *L.J. Turley at home in Central City, Kentucky*
Bottom: *Our Ordinance Division at one of our reunions. Front row–Scotty Parrish and Jim Snellen. Back row–Ed Przybyl, Charlie Rosen, Tom Ball, Justin "Gene" Carlock, and Don Mericle.*

Top Left: *Captain Chester.*
Top Right: *Turley & Captain Chester.*
Bottom: *1996 reunion in Williamsburg, Virginia. (Left to right) L. J. Turley, Dot Snellen, Mrs. Nanadiego, Jim Snellen, B/Gen. Tagumpay A. Nanadiego from the Philippine, Embassy in Washington, D.C., and Captain Alvin P. Chester.*

Top: *Captain Alvin P. Chester received the Philippine Liberation Medal from B/Gen. Tagumpay A. Nanadiego from the Philippine Embassy in Washington, D.C. General Nanadiego was in the Bataan Death March in the Philippines.*
Bottom: *2004 reunion. Walter J. Maki, former Radioman, 2ⁿᵈ Class on the left–L. J. Turley on the right.*

Appendix

My story is not only about myself, but also about my ship, the USS Cofer. She earned eight battle stars during her service. As I am writing this memoir of my time in the Navy, I am consulting the ship's complete log. A brief history of the USS Cofer before my arrival should be included...

Originally built as a DE (Destroyer Escort), the USS Cofer (DE-208) was launched on September 6, 1944 and was christened on January 19, 1944 (eight months before I was assigned to her). Christening the Cofer was Mrs. Mary Jane Cofer, mother of the late John Joseph Cofer, Seaman, First Class, who died a hero's death on November 13, 1942 in the Battle of Guadalcanal in the South Pacific. He was a rangefinder operator who was awarded the Silver Star for his gallant and intrepid conduct aboard the USS Aaron Ward (DD-483). The Cofer christening took place in the Navy yard in Charleston, South Carolina where she was built.

The Commanding Officer was Lieutenant Commander Alvin P. Chester, USNR, former Commanding Officer of the USS EC Daily (DE-17). Captain Chester was the Cofer's skipper until December 18, 1944, when he was relieved by his Executive Officer, Lt. Herbert C. McClees, USNR. At commissioning, Lt. Charles H. Cofer (who was a brother of the deceased John Joseph Cofer) was also aboard the USS Cofer.

The USS Cofer (DE-208) was 306 feet long and normally held 12 officers and 190 enlisted men. She had one 3-inch 50-caliber gun, 40-mm guns, 20-mm guns, torpedoes, and depth charges. She was originally built to escort troop ships, merchant ships, and others across the Atlantic Ocean. Her role would normally be to zigzag in front, at the sides, and behind a convoy of ships to protect the slow-moving liberty ships carrying supplies to Europe, Russia, and other Atlantic destinations against the German U-boats. The Cofer's screening position was normally the lucky #13, but occasionally she would relieve another DE (Destroyer Escort), so that ship could refuel while under way with the convoy. Under extreme conditions, the Cofer really served as a submarine chaser. The crew constantly searched for the unseen underwater enemy—the German submarine, which had wreaked havoc on Allied shipping.

While on duty, the Officer on Deck would log all of the daily events during his duty in the ship's log. The Captain later signed off on each day's 24-hour period. The following passages are taken from the Cofer's log which was recorded every 4 hours...

Wednesday—January 19, 1944
A pilot came aboard the USS Cofer to navigate the ship up the Cooper River in Charleston, South Carolina and completed his duty in about an hour, turning the ship over to Captain Chester and Lieutenant McClees. The pilot returned on January 28th to guide the Cofer down the Cooper River.

Wednesday—February 2, 1994
The Cofer performed her first cruising and firing tests.

Sunday—February 13, 1944
Finally, the Cofer made her first true trip to sea, en route for Charleston, South Carolina and on to Bermuda. This was most of the sailors' first trip and was considered a "shakedown cruise." For the next few weeks, along with the USS Holder (DE-401), the Cofer made wartime shakedown cruises off Bermuda almost daily. Performing gunnery exercises were a main focus during these cruises.

Thursday—March 9, 1944
Almost a month later, the Cofer was now ready for war-cruising in the Atlantic—ready to search for German U-boats. The USS Holder and the Cofer left Bermuda, heading back to Charleston, South Carolina. While en route, the crew, under Captain Chester's direction, made daily inspections and drills of guns and magazines, as well as depth charge drills because these were the U-boat's greatest threat. The Captain wanted everything ready if, and when, needed.

Saturday—March 11, 1944
The Cofer arrived back in the Charleston, South Carolina Navy Yard after completing her training mission to and around Bermuda. This same day, more than one-third of the men and several officers left the ship for leaves of up to six days. The Cofer was put in dry dock for hull, rudder, etc. inspections and all appeared normal. A number of the enlisted men turned up late from leave and the Captain assigned punishment accordingly on March 18th.

Monday—March 20, 1944
This was the day the officers and men had been waiting and working toward. The Cofer left Charleston, South Carolina for New York under war-cruising conditions. The gun crews went through many drills, just to be ready when needed. The ship arrived the next day at the Brooklyn Navy Yard.

Thursday—March 23, 1944
At 0400 hours, the Cofer left Brooklyn for her first wartime duty. During a heavy storm, one seaman was injured after being thrown against the ship's bulkhead.

Friday—March 24, 1944
The Cofer was finally underway and headed across the Atlantic to Gibraltar off the Iberian Peninsula, continually exercising at General Quarters. When called to General Quarters, the crew was called over the ship's intercom to prepare to enter battle. In addition to sailors on duty, all off-duty or sleeping crewmembers must be at their battle stations when General Quarters was called.

Saturday—March 25, 1944
The Cofer continued toward Gibraltar, now escorting a convoy of ships sailing at about 16 knots, which was considered a standard speed. The Captain held mast and assigned punishment for several men who were late returning from liberty when on leave in New York.

Monday—March 27, 1944
The Destroyers and Destroyer Escorts in the convoy continued having daily gun exercises.

Saturday—April 1, 1944
After eleven days of sailing, the Cofer and the task force finally arrived at Gibraltar and all shipmates felt relieved, as they had safely completed their first Atlantic crossing. When moored in Gibraltar, the Cofer noted various US, British, French, Dutch, and Australian ships afloat.

Thursday—April 6, 1944
The Cofer left Gibraltar for Hampton Roads, Virginia—back to the "good old USA". All shipmates were ready to return home, but they knew going back across the Atlantic was a dangerous task. The destroyer escorts and destroyers did their screening to protect their convoy of ships with all guns and depth charges ready. There were 1,755 various types of ships in the convoy—some convoy! They had one false scare the first day underway.

Friday—April 7, 1944
This is the first time the Cofer received mail from home from the USS Nelson (DD-623).

Thursday–April 20, 1944
The convoy continued moving at a slow 9 to 9.5 knots, screening to protect the slower convoy. The Cofer was told to drop back and relieve the USS Herndon (DD-638), who had been escorting a Norwegian steamer, the S.S. Pan Aruba, which was lagging 12 miles behind the convoy.

Saturday–April 22, 1944
Finally, after a very slow Atlantic crossing, the Cofer was diverted to the Brooklyn Navy Yard in New York. A number of the men were given short leaves.

Wednesday–May 3, 1944
The Cofer left the Brooklyn Navy Yard for Casco Bay, Maine in a convoy waiting for further orders. At 1415 hours, she anchored in Casco Bay, Maine.

Monday–May 8, 1944
The Cofer left Casco Bay, Maine at 0751 hours for Yorktown, Virginia.

Wednesday–May 10, 1944
Arrived at Yorktown at 1052 hours to pick up depth charges. Later, at 1300 hours, the Cofer left for Norfolk, Virginia while awaiting further orders and arrived in Norfolk at 1630 hours.

Saturday–May 13, 1944
Today the Cofer left for another Atlantic crossing heading for the northern parts of Africa, escorting a large convoy of ships with average speeds of 9.5 knots.

Wednesday–May 17, 1944
The Cofer had to drop back and stand by a straggler ship, the S.S. Winfield Smith, which had engine troubles. The Cofer circled and circled the Winfield, screening 2,000 to 3,000 yards around the Winfield at 12 knots. The Cofer was determined to protect this disabled ship until the necessary engine repairs could be completed. While screening the disabled ship, the Cofer was the only war ship protecting the disabled liberty ship. Both were dangerously exposed to the German U-boats, but that is what the escort ships were designed to do. Around 0900 hours, the necessary repairs were completed and the Winfield and the Cofer increased speeds to return to the large convoy. Four hours later, the Cofer and Winfield reached the convoy.

Almost daily the convoy ships went to General Quarters, conducting every known exercise drill such as underwater sonar drills, tracking air targets, and practicing firing every gun on the ship. The largest gun was the 3-inch 50-caliber located on the forward section of the bridge. The Cofer sometimes even practiced abandoning ship, as this was the most common conflict in the Atlantic crossings due to the U-boat activities.

Depth charges were the most effective means of destroying U-boats while sonar was the most effective way of pin pointing U-boats' locations underwater. This was done by sending sound waves out that bounced off the U-boats. Before the depth charges could be launched however, the crewmember in charge of the depth charges had to insert the small red detonators, which would cause the depth charge to explode.

Friday—May 19, 1944
After the usual test-firing exercises under battle station conditions, all was secure and a captain's mast was held. 50 hours of extra duty were awarded to five enlisted men for standing improper watch. The Captain insisted on each officer and man doing his part, and then some. So when someone failed to stand watch properly, the captain was tough—and he was respected tremendously for this. As he would say, failing to do your part could cost many lives or account for the loss of the ship. So, if you were on watch, you had better be alert and fulfill your responsibilities or else you would answer to Captain Alvin P. Chester. He was nice, but tough, when he had to be. Captain Alvin Chester was a stickler for readiness and nobody could fault him for this. His belief was to train to be ready in a minute's notice.

This was Captain Chester's second Destroyer Escort duty, and he knew what was what. The crew was so proud to have an experienced battle-tested captain in charge of the ship. Most of these officers and men, this was their first experience at sea.

Monday—May 22, 1944
Today was a typical day, still cruising and screening at 9.5 knots. An underwater contact was made and General Quarters was sounded, but it was identified as a large whale. Then another contact by radar was made, General Quarters sounded and, as required, all hands went to man their battle stations. This happens within minutes—the men sleep in their clothes and everything except their shoes. The troops must be at their assigned battle stations within minutes or sooner, if possible. This radar contact turned out to be a Swedish ship.

Sunday—May 28, 1944
Received mail from the USS Newman (DE-205). At 1501 hours, General

Quarters was sounded as another ship reported a torpedo had been heard. This was later identified as hydrostatic noise. Later in the day the convoy's speeds reduced to 7 knots.

Monday—May 29, 1944
The next morning, convoy speeds increased to 8 knots, which was still so much slower than the 23 knots the Cofer was capable of cruising. However, the liberty ships were not capable of traveling as fast as the Cofer.

Wednesday—June 1, 1944
Up until now, the crossing had been uneventful until the Cofer identified some wreckage at sea. The Escort Commander instructed the Cofer to drop depth charges at 1310 hours. Three were fired directly at the wreckage. No debris or change was noticed, so the Cofer returned to its screening station after securing from General Quarters. At 2150 hours, the Cofer left her screening station to investigate an unidentified ship astern, which proved to be a tugboat towing a ship and an armed trawler. All secured from General Quarters and the Cofer returned to screening the convoy.

Friday—June 2, 1944
The convoy entered the channel at Baie de Bizerte, Tunisia in northern Africa and dropped anchor at 1633 hours. Various US, British, and French Navy ships were present at anchor plus many Allied merchant ships. As the engine and fire rooms were held in standby conditions, the Cofer remained at war-cruising and anchor watches.

Saturday—June 10, 1944
Received orders at 1440 hours to get under way as soon as possible for the United States. By 1508 hours, the ship got underway to join a new convoy.

Sunday—June 11, 1944
Received mail from the USS Liddle (DE-206).

Monday—June 16, 1944
Merchant ships from Algiers joined the convoy while four others left.

Tuesday—June 17, 1944
The Cofer received orders to screen a straggler, the SS Malplaquet, to assist her in proceeding independently to Oran, Algeria. After one hour, the mission was

completed and the Cofer returned to her convoy.

Friday—June 23, 1944
While underway, the Cofer left her station to refuel from the tanker Cowaneque (AO-79). It took forty minutes to refuel at sea.

Monday—June 26, 1944
Still underway, the Cofer was ordered to investigate a radar contact 9 miles astern. It was found to be a straggler, #126 of the convoy.

Thursday—June 29, 1944
The Cofer arrived in Gravesano Bay, New York and then proceeded to Sandy Hook, New Jersey to unload ammunition and make preparations to transform the ship. The DE ships like the Cofer had quickly proved their worth during the war. In fact, there were hundreds of DEs (Destroyer Escorts) built during the war. As the war progressed, however, a number of the DEs, including the Cofer, were later converted to APDs (Attack Personnel Destroyer—later renamed as "Armed Personnel Destroyers") for fast transport of assault troops as well as convoy escorts.

Friday—June 30, 1944
The Cofer proceeded to Pier #2 in the Todd Shipyard in Brooklyn, New York for her conversion from the DE-208 to the APD-62. During the conversion, torpedo tubes were removed from Cofer and the deck was raised to add 140 additional troop quarters.

While at Todd Shipyard, many men were transferred, including Captain Alvin P. Chester, for temporary duty elsewhere until the ship's conversion was completed. Some of these men were sent to receiving barracks in the Navy Yard in Brooklyn; others to the amphibious training center in Lido Beach, New York; many to Naval Training Station in Norfolk, Virginia; some to the Naval Boiler and Turbine Laboratory in Philadelphia, Pennsylvania; and many to the anti-aircraft training center in Prices Neck, Rhode Island. After these men completed their temporary assignments, most were given a 20-day leave. When they returned, all were assigned to temporary barracks in New York while awaiting the conversion completion.

Thursday—August 31, 1944
Commander William S. Parsons, USN, assumed command of the Com Trans Division #103 and he was assigned to the USS Newman (APD-59). Division #103

was the Cofer's new division of ships made up of the USS Newman (APD-59), USS Liddle (APD-60), USS Kepldart (APD-61), USS Cofer (APD-62), and USS Lloyd (APD-63).

This is the history of a great ship that, as a Destroyer Escort and Attack Personnel Destroyer, earned eight battle stars. Out of all 570 ships receiving battle stars, only six DE and APD ships received more battle stars than the Cofer.

Printed in the United States
by Baker & Taylor Publisher Services